Albert Bandura

DIALOGUES IN CONTEMPORARY PSYCHOLOGY SERIES

Richard I. Evans, Series Editor

DIALOGUE WITH GORDON ALLPORT

DIALOGUE WITH ERIK ERIKSON

DIALOGUE WITH ERICH FROMM

DIALOGUE WITH C. G. JUNG

DIALOGUE WITH R. D. LAING

DIALOGUE WITH JEAN PIAGET

DIALOGUE WITH CARL ROGERS

DIALOGUE WITH B. F. SKINNER

PSYCHOLOGY AND ARTHUR MILLER

ALBERT BANDURA: THE MAN AND HIS
IDEAS—A DIALOGUE

Albert Bandura:
The Man and
His Ideas—
A Dialogue

Richard I. Evans

Foreword by
Ernest R. Hilgard

New York
Westport, Connecticut
London

Library of Congress Cataloging-in-Publication Data

Evans, Richard I. (Richard Isadore), 1922–
    Albert Bandura: the man and his ideas—a dialogue / Richard
I. Evans.
        p.   cm.—(Dialogues in contemporary psychology)
    Bibliography: p.
    "Bibliography of Albert Bandura": p.
    Includes index.
    ISBN 0–275–93352–0 (alk. paper)
    1. Bandura, Albert, 1925–   —Interviews. 2. Psychologists—
United States—Interviews. 3. Psychology—United States—History.
I. Bandura, Albert, 1925–   . II. Title. III. Series: Evans,
Richard I. (Richard Isadore), 1922–   Dialogues in contemporary
psychology.
BF109.B28E95   1989
150'.92—dc20   89–32273

Library of Congress Catalog Card Number: 89–32273
ISBN: 0–275–93352–0

First published in 1989

Praeger Publishers, One Madison Avenue, New York, NY 10010
A division of Greenwood Press, Inc.

Printed in the United States of America

∞

The paper used in this book complies with the
Permanent Paper Standard issued by the National
Information Standards Organization (Z39.48-1984).

10 9 8 7 6 5 4 3 2 1

TO MY LOVELY
WIFE ZENA WHO
HAS DEMONSTRATED
REMARKABLE SELF-EFFICACY
IN COPING WITH AN
ILLNESS; AND TO ALL
OF OUR CHILDREN.
THEY HAVE
DEMONSTRATED
SUCH EXTRAORDINARY
SUPPORT.

Contents

Foreword by Ernest R. Hilgard   ix

Preface: Perspective on the Dialogue
Style and Content   xiii

Acknowledgments   xvii

**Personal Background and Early
Contributions**   1

Aggression and Violence   19

**Moral Development and Moral
Disengagement**   39

Self-Efficacy   51

Reactions to Criticism, A Recent Book   81

References   87

Bibliography: Works of Albert Bandura   91

Index   109

Foreword

When Albert Bandura received one of the Awards for Distinguished Scientific Contributions to Psychology from the American Psychological Foundation in 1980, his citation read in part as follows:

For masterful modeling as researcher, teacher, and theoretician. He has sparked renewed interest in covert events. He has led the profession in explicating the social, symbolic, and self-regulatory determinants of meaningful learning and behavior change. He has exemplified and fostered innovative experiments on a host of topics including moral development, observational learning, fear acquisition, treatment strategies, self-control, standard setting, self-referent processes, and the cognitive regulation of behavior. . . . His vigor, warmth, and human example have inspired his many students' own self-efficacy. (*American Psychologist*, 1981, *36*, 27).

Having been his colleague since his arrival at Stanford as an assistant professor in 1953, with the strong support of Robert Sears, then department head, who had kept in touch with the

University of Iowa, I can attest to his qualities in all these respects, as they are revealed also in the dialogue reported here, supplementing the earlier one that was published by Dr. Evans, in 1976.

He was born December 4, 1925, in northern Alberta, and graduated from the University of British Columbia, which later recognized him as a distinguished alumnus by awarding him the honorary Doctor of Science degree. He did his graduate study at the University of Iowa, where he received the Ph.D. under Arthur Benton in 1952. As a student of clinical psychology he interned for a year at the Wichita Guidance Center before coming to Stanford. At Stanford he moved up through the ranks to become a full professor, to serve as department chairman, and to be honored by being awarded an endowed chair.

His many years as a productive researcher and theoretician, as author of scores of articles and numerous books, were crowned by a major opus that appeared in 1986, *Social Foundations of Thought and Action: A Social Cognitive Theory*. In 10 insightful chapters he places his own theory in the context of other models of human nature and causality, and deals thoughtfully with each of the major emphases that he has supported: observational learning based on modeling, enactive learning, social diffusion and innovation, predictive knowledge and forethought, incentive and vicarious motivators, self-regulatory mechanisms, self-efficacy, and cognitive regulators. He is able to cite his own work and that of his students on these topics, but draws widely on other supporting studies in the some 2,000 references that he cites.

In his major book he has taken the opportunity to expand on his concept of reciprocal determinism, in the special form of triadic reciprocity. Reciprocal determinism begins with the concept that persons and situations affect each other, so that they are not independent, and we cannot assign some percent of responsibility to each. The triadic conception enlarges the set of interactions to allow interactions between behavior (B), cognitive and other personal factors (P), and environmental influences (E). The same events, wherever they belong in this scheme, may change their status in different contexts. Hence his use of the word *determinism* does not imply that events are completely determined by a prior sequence of causes. Without espousing a doctrine of free will, the freedom from prior causes is accepted on a heuristic basis, as in his discussion of the significance of chance encounters. To what extent "chance" encounters are free of prior causes can be debated on metaphysical grounds, but in daily life they are indeed unplanned and unpredictable. The word "will" does not appear in the index, but of course "self-reflectivity" and "self-efficacy" serve the same purposes that the concept of will once served.

Bandura's status in psychology has been widely recognized by his fellow psychologists in the honors and awards that he has received. He had received a distinguished scientific achievement award from the Division of Clinical Psychology of the American Psychological Association, and a Distinguished Scientist Award from the California State Psychological Association, before receiving the national award cited above. He was elected to the presidency of the American Psychological Association in 1974 and was president of the Western Psychological Association in 1980. Other awards have gone beyond psychology, as in the Guggenheim Fellowship in 1972, and his Distinguished Contribution Award from the International Society for Research on Aggression in 1980. He was in that year elected as a fellow of the American Academy of Arts and Sciences. In 1989, he was elected to the Institute of Medicine of the National Academy of Sciences. This list is not complete, but it suffices to indicate the acclaim that he has received over the years.

It is well that we have this book to give in his own words how he views his life and experience as a psychologist. The accompanying visual presentation of the interview helps to bring out his personal qualities better than I can depict them in words. I am pleased to have been invited to add these few words of introduction to this volume, which features one of the leading psychologists of our time.

Ernest R. Hilgard
Stanford University

Preface: Perspective on the Dialogue Style and Content

This volume constitutes the fourteenth in a series based on dialogues with some of the world's outstanding contributors to psychology. To avoid possible misunderstanding about the goals of the dialogue style used in this volume, some perspective may be of value. Designed, it is hoped, as an innovative teaching device, the series was launched in 1957 with completion of filmed and audiotaped dialogues with the late C. G. Jung and Ernest Jones, supported by a grant from the Fund for the Advancement of Education. The series was continued under a grant from the National Science Foundation. A basic purpose of the project remains to produce, for teaching purposes, a series of films and books that introduce the viewer to our most creative contributors to the field of psychology and human behavior. We hope that these films and books may also serve as documents of increasing value in the history of the behavioral sciences.[1]

The books in this series are based on edited transcripts of the dialogue, including audiotaped discussions as well as the audio portion of the films. These dialogues are designed to introduce the reader to the contributor's major ideas and points of view, conveying through the extemporaneousness of the dialogue style a feeling for the personality of the contributor. We would hope that dialogues with outstanding contributors as they seriously examine their own work, will be no less significant by virtue of their informality. Such dialogues as a novel "primary source" might be one means of stimulating students, who too frequently rely on secondary sources to learn about our seminal contributors to psychology, to pursue primary sources.

A more detailed description of the philosophy and techniques of this project is reported elsewhere (Kathleen Fisher, 1983, Evans 1969c). However, a few points bearing on the content of these volumes can be emphasized here. The questions are intended to reflect the published writings of the interviewee and the perspective of the interviewee on other provocative issues or concepts in psychology. As indicated earlier, as a novel "primary source" of the contributor's ideas, it is hoped that these dialogues stimulate the viewer or reader to go back to the original writings of the contributor, which develop more fully the ideas presented through our dialogue. In fact, at least one investigation of the impact of these dialogues (Evans, *Dialogue with C. G. Jung*, 1981) would appear to support this effect of at least one of these dialogues.

The term dialogue instead of conversation or discussion was chosen to describe these interchanges, because dialogue may imply a more programmed content. Dialogue, however, also implies a challenge of, or confrontation with, the individual being interviewed. To some, the term may also suggest that the interviewer is using the individual being interviewed as a tool to project the interviewer's objectives. My goals here would preclude either of these interpretations. It is my intention that these dialogues reflect a constructive method of instruction, with my role as interviewer being that of a mediator, neither that of the center of focus nor of the critical challenger. I believe it is within the spirit of these teaching aims of the project that our contributors so generously agree to participate.

As was the case with subjects of the earlier books in the series, Jung and Jones (Evans, *Dialogue with C. G. Jung*, 1981), Fromm (Evans, *Dialogue with Erich Fromm*, 1981), Erikson (Evans, *Dialogue with Erik Erikson*, 1981), Skinner (Evans, *Dialogue with B. F. Skinner*, 1981), Arthur Miller (Evans, *Psychology and Arthur Miller*, 1981), Allport[2] (Evans, *Dialogue with Gordon Allport*, 1981), Piaget (Evans, *Dialogue with Jean Piaget*, 1981), Rogers (Evans, *Dialogue with Carl Rogers*, 1981), and Lorenz (Evans, *Konrad Lorenz: The Man and His Ideas*, 1975), Laing (Evans, *Dialogue with R. D. Laing*, 1981), it is hoped that the dialogue presentation allows the reader to be introduced to, or to reexamine, some of Albert Bandura's ideas through this relatively extemporaneous interchange. It should be pointed out, however, that in his writings, as Bandura expresses himself in his own unique style, he has the opportunity to rewrite and polish until he deems the finished product satisfactory. In the spontaneity of our discussion, even though he was given an opportunity to edit its content, he is called upon to develop his ideas extemporaneously. As suggested earlier, I hope that this element may present more of Bandura's perspective as a person while losing none of the ideas central to his thoughts. As was also indicated earlier, in the case of this book as well as in the others in the series, some editorial license was exercised to shift effectively from oral to printed communication in the service of accuracy, readability, clarity, and grammatical construction. However, the dialogue presented here duplicates, insofar as possible, the essence of the exchange between Albert Bandura and myself as it actually took place. We hope that this dialogue presents a useful supplement to Bandura's more formally written work, and stimulates the reader to probe more deeply into Bandura's rich and provocative array of ideas by reading his published papers and books.

NOTES

1. The films are distributed by PCR, Audio-Visual Services, Pennsylvania State University, Special Services Building, University Park, Pennsylvania 16802.

2. *Gordon Allport: The Man and His Ideas* received the 1971 American Psychological Foundation Media Award in the Book category.

Acknowledgments

In the process involved in filming and audiotaping the dialogues with Albert Bandura and transcribing, editing, and integrating them into the present volume, I am indebted to a great many individuals. Although space prohibits mentioning everyone who so kindly assisted me in this venture, I wish to express my appreciation to at least some of them.

First of all, I am grateful for the support of the National Science Foundation, without which this project could not have been implemented. Many thanks to Rice University Media Center Director Brian Huberman with the assistance of Phil Davis who both functioned in the demanding roles of technical director and film editor for the filmed sections of this dialogue which provided some of the content for this volume. Thanks also to my office manager Lois Parker and to Nancy Crossland for transcribing all the original audiotapes of my several hours of discussion with Dr. Bandura.

Working with this transcribed discussion, I am indebted to Susan A. Anderson and Thomas J. Benner for completing a content analysis within a structure I provided, and some initial editing of the dialogue material. Thomas Benner then did a splendid job of further integrating and editing this material as he assisted me in completing the first draft.

After Social Psychology doctoral student Rock L. Clapper assisted me in extensive editing of the draft, Lois Parker, working with Donna Schmidt, did a splendid job of integrating all of these revisions into the word processor. Finally, after still further editing, Lois Parker integrated the final draft into the word processor. Rock Clapper also proved to be an excellent proofreader and provided reference checks throughout this process.

For his fine introduction, thanks are accorded to Ernest J. Hilgard of Stanford University (who in fact served on the initial Advisory Committee of this project, Dialogues with Distinguished Contributors to Psychology, of which this volume is a part).

Finally, the wonderful cooperation of Albert Bandura cannot be emphasized enough. Not only was he willing to participate in the several hours of filming and audiotaping sessions and discuss the format of this volume, but he spent additional time in exhaustively editing his component of the dialogue content. His genuine kindness, good humor, and stimulating insights contributed greatly to my efforts in preparing this volume in addition to his substantive responses to my questions as the dialogue proceeded.

Albert Bandura

1

Personal Background and Early Contributions

In this section, Dr. Bandura and I discuss his psychological training at the University of British Columbia and State University at Iowa, and how he was influenced by the logical positivism and behaviorism which were pervasive during the Kenneth Spence era at Iowa, and how his concept of cognitive behaviorism emerged. We then discuss what influenced the development of his work on modeling. Finally, we discuss how he developed and applied an empirical, theory-based approach to psychotherapy.

As background for this section, a brief biographical sketch of Dr. Bandura to supplement Ernest Hilgard's foreword might be appropriate. Albert Bandura is David Starr Jordan Professor of Social Sciences in Psychology at Stanford University. He is a proponent of social cognitive theory. This theory accords a central role to cognitive, vicarious, self-regulatory and self-reflective processes in sociocognitive functioning. His recent book, Social Foundations of Thought and Action: A Social Cognitive Theory, *provides the conceptual framework and analyzes the large body of knowledge bearing on this theory. Bandura is past president of the American Psychological Association and the recipient of its Distinguished Scientific Contributions Award. A bibliography of his published works appears at the end of this volume.*

EVANS: To begin our discussion, Dr. Bandura, perhaps you would like to talk a little bit about what influenced you to become a psychologist.

BANDURA: Your question raises an interesting issue. I have come to the view that some of the most important determinants of career and life paths often occur through the most trivial of circumstances. In looking back I can see some fortuitous elements in how I got inducted into psychology. As an undergraduate at the University of British Columbia, I commuted with a group of pre-meds and engineers who were very early risers. So I found myself filling a gap in my schedule by taking a psychology course. I became fascinated with the subject matter, especially the clinical aspects.

EVANS: Of course you went on to the University of Iowa to complete your Ph.D. in Clinical Psychology. What led to that decision?

BANDURA: At that time I felt strongly that a responsible Clinical Psychology should be founded on a reliable knowledge base. We should not be subjecting people to treatments and then, some years later, trying to figure out what effects they have. We should test treatments before we embark on widespread applications. When it came time to choose a graduate school, I asked my adviser, "Where are the stone tablets of psychology?" He pointed me to Iowa's renowned graduate program, but with a warning that it was a tough place. I found Iowa to be intellectually lively, but also very supportive. So I wrote to my adviser that my initial experiences at Iowa reminded me of Mark Twain who once said of Wagner's music, "It's not as bad as it sounds!" At Iowa we were imprinted early on a model of scholarship that combined high respect for theory linked to venturesome research. It was an excellent beginning for a career.

EVANS: Among your various contributions, your theory of modeling appears to be quite significant. I wonder if you might talk about how Miller and Dollard's book, *Social Learning and*

Imitation (1941), contributed to the development of your theory of modeling.

BANDURA: I was attracted to Miller and Dollard's work as an alternative to the prevailing theory of learning, which assumed that people acquire competencies and new patterns of behavior through response consequences. I could not imagine how a culture could ever transmit its language, its mores and all the complex competencies that are required to function effectively, through this tedious trial and error process. It would take three or four lifetimes just to master basic skills. In real life, of course, errors can maim and kill, so acquiring competencies entirely through the effects of one's actions has tremendous hazards. It made sense to short-cut this tedious and hazardous process by providing competent models. If you wanted to teach someone how to drive an automobile, you would provide a competent model of how to do it. Trial and error could have disastrous consequences for both the driver and the environment. I was attracted to Miller and Dollard's work on the assumption that human development requires a much more powerful mode of transmitting competencies than does trial and error.

EVANS: How did you proceed to conceptualize modeling?

BANDURA: Several different constructs had been applied to the modeling process. First, there is the notion of imitation. In imitation, a person copies exactly what he or she sees the model doing. Social mimicry would have a very limited effect. Second, there is the more global and diffuse construct of identification that was part of Freudian theory. This construct was concerned with the wholesale incorporation of personality patterns. I felt that imitation was much too narrow and identification was much too nebulous and diffuse to serve the purpose of scientific inquiry. So I began to develop the notion of modeling as a broad phenomenon that serves diverse functions. This conceptualization of modeling is concerned more with observers' extracting the rules and structure of behavior, rather than just copying particular examples they had observed. For example, in language learning, children are extracting the rules of how to speak grammatically rather than just imitating particular sentences. Once they acquire the structure and the rules, they can use that knowledge to generate new patterns of behavior that go beyond what they've seen or heard. As they acquire the rules of language, they can generate sentences they have never heard. So modeling is a much more complex abstract process than a simple process of response mimicry. I became interested in the multiple functions that modeling serves. Through modeling we can transmit skills, attitudes, values, and emotional proclivities. This is the acquisition function—the teaching function of modeling.

Modeling can also reduce or strengthen inhibitions over pre-existing behavior. If people observe a model's action resulting in punishing consequences, this discourages them from using that pattern of behavior. However, if they observe that modeling results in positive consequences, this encourages them to adopt similar behavior. This is the second function of modeling, namely, its inhibitory and disinhibitory function.

EVANS: Your third function of models referred to models of social behavior in which nothing new was required. Is that correct?

BANDURA: Yes, this is the social facilitation function. In this process no new competencies are being acquired and inhibitions affected serve as social guides. The whole fashion and taste industry relies on that modeling function.

EVANS: As you expanded the function of modeling, what followed?

BANDURA: I became impressed with the growing power of the symbolic environment in shaping human thought, affect and action. We have seen a communications revolution in which television, combined with satellite transmission, has greatly expanded the speed and scope of human influence. Most peoples' images of reality on which they base many of their actions are shaped by what they see and hear rather than by their own direct experiences. If we relied solely on direct experience, we would have a very limited experiential base for acquiring many of our attitudes, beliefs and competencies. This is because in our daily routines, we travel restricted routes, going to the same places, seeing the same set of friends and associates. So in terms of direct experience, our information is very limited, but we have images about realities that we have never experienced personally. These views are formed on the basis of televised representations of society and human relationships. Symbolic modeling influences are shaping the attitudes and beliefs of people much more profoundly. Televised modeling has greatly accelerated the social diffusion of ideas, both within a society and from one society to another. Now we have almost instant diffusion of information.

If you examine our psychological theories, most of them were cast long before this tremendous technological revolution in communications. This is true whether you consider Watsonian or Skinnerian behaviorism, Freudian, Adlerian, or Jungian psychodynamic theories, or Piagetian theory. These theories do not encompass the tremendous power of the symbolic environment from which people now are acquiring much of their knowledge. Symbolic modeling is playing an important role in shaping our images of reality. A theory of psychology should be in step with our social realities. We need to have a theory that acknowledges that the modes of human influence have been altered radically by these revolutionary changes. The psychological principles operate similarly, but the mode of conveyance has greatly changed. These changes should be reflected in our theories of human behavior.

EVANS: Another major area of your contributions relates to the concept of aggression. Could you discuss how you approached aggression?

BANDURA: Let me address this issue in several ways. First, theories of aggression: There are three main theories. One is the instinct theory. Freud (1933) postulated a death instinct that keeps generating itself and must be periodically discharged by venting aggression in one form or another. Konrad Lorenz (1966) postulated a fighting instinct. That, too, generates itself spontaneously and requires periodic discharge. No one has been able to find such a biological aggression-producing mechanism. So I had considerable reservations about a theory that puts such a heavy emphasis on instinctual control of aggression.

The second theory is the frustration-aggression theory. In this view you do not have an instinct generating aggressive energy, but rather environmental conditions of frustration produce an aggressive drive. But the frustration-aggression theory was not all that different from the instinct theory in terms of its social implications. Since frustration is ever-present, people are burdened with frustration which must be periodically discharged by some form of aggression.

EVANS: It was then that you developed your social learning model, wasn't it?

BANDURA: Yes. Although the frustration-aggression theory was the dominant theory at the time, it ran into difficulties under close experimental scrutiny. Frustration could produce any variety of reactions and one does not need frustration to get aggression. I began to work on the social learning model of aggression. This theory assumes that aggression has multiple sources; it can be instigated by a variety of conditions and it can serve multiple purposes.

A comprehensive theory must explain acquisition of aggressive styles of behavior. If there is any behavior where observational learning is important, it is aggression, because ineffectual aggression can get one disfigured, maimed or killed. One cannot afford to learn through trial and error. So most aggressive patterns are transmitted through modeling.

EVANS: So you could see modeling as a critical factor at the acquisition end of aggression, particularly through exposure to symbolic media.

BANDURA: I doubt that most people have ever witnessed a homicide or vicious beating. But by the time children reach kindergarten, they have probably witnessed every imaginable form of human atrocity through exposure to the symbolic media.

One would not teach military recruits how to lob grenades through trial and error. This mode of learning would create a situation of, "Look, sergeant, no arms." It would give new meaning to the wartime movie, "A Farewell to Arms." When you have a behavior that can produce dangerous consequences, you transmit it through modeling and perfect it under simulated conditions. That is why I emphasized modeling as a basic mode of transmission. People do not come equipped with aggressive skills. They have to develop them.

EVANS: As you moved into the field from your initial training in clinical psychology, you, of course, like many clinical psychologists, were interested in psychotherapy. You were aware of the work of the Skinnerians and the phrase "behavior modification" that emerged. You then wrote a book *Principles of Behavior Modification* (Bandura, 1969) that began to look at a view of behavior modification which really began to incorporate some of your social learning conceptions. The book obviously was very influential and it seemed to have predated a lot of the increasing movement toward what was later called "cognitive behavior modification." I think it was probably the very first work that reconsidered mental processes as directed toward what appeared to be a bit too sterile on emphasis on the behavior itself.

BANDURA: In this book I emphasized the influential role played by cognitive, modeling and self-regulatory processes in human motivation and action.

EVANS: I was wondering about how you happened to move in this direction and how this was received. What kind of reaction did you get from some of the more radical behaviorists?

BANDURA: Well, let me begin by providing a context. In the 1950s, a large number of outcome studies were published showing that it was difficult to demonstrate much of a difference between treated and non-treated groups, particularly on stringent criteria, such as actual change in psychosocial functioning. Treatment looked a bit better on self-report measures of change. People felt they got something out of it. But on stringent psychosocial measures of functioning, the outcome data were not too encouraging. I concluded that there was a basic problem in the mode of change that was being used. The treatments relied heavily on the interview as the basic vehicle of personality change. It was assumed that by analyzing people's reports of the problems they're experiencing and the problems they're reenacting with the therapist, they would gain insight into the inner dynamics of their behavior patterns. They would learn new ways, and self-insight would produce behavior change. People were gaining all kinds of insights, but not changing their behavior all that much.

It is easier to change people's beliefs about the causes of troublesome behavior than it is to change their troublesome behavior. For example, it's easier to convince an alcoholic that he drinks because he was fixated orally than to have him give up booze. I began to have serious questions as to whether the interview was a powerful enough vehicle for a personality change. The more effective way of producing change was to create conditions that enabled people to acquire new competencies and to gain mastery experiences. This is a much more action-oriented treatment centered on having people confront the problems they were facing and helping them to acquire more effective ways of managing and coping with them.

There was a general move in the field away from the psychodynamic model of psychopathology. It assumed a thorough psychic determinism. But it involved a very loose causal linkage. You had a mental life that was largely unconscious and could produce any kind of behavior. It could even produce opposite forms of behavior. For example, a hostile impulse could produce aggression or sweetness. Try to verify that kind of theory! It was founded on a cause by a psychic life that could not predict anything very specific.

This theory also embraced a quasi-disease model in which problem behavior was supposedly a symptom of underlying pathology. But it was not a neurophysiological pathology. It was a psychic pathology. So you had a metaphoric disease producing symptoms. The interview was the basic vehicle for changing the unconscious psychic determinant. I was coming to the view that to increase the power and predictability of treatment would require a mastery-oriented approach to human problems. So my students and I were developing a mastery modeling approach as the vehicle for change. It turned out to be a powerful mode of change.

At that time, of course, other approaches were being developed as an alternative to the psychodynamic treatment. There are three different approaches that come under the rubric of behavior modification. These approaches are not worshipped at the same theoretical altar. The Skinnerians adopted a model of environmental determinism in which behavior is shaped and controlled by the environment. In this approach to treatment, to change behavior, you have to change the environmental contingencies. Thought is epiphenomenal, so it does not influence behavior. Proponents of Skinner's approach try to effect change by altering the environment.

Social cognitive theory presents a cognitive interactional model of human functioning. In this approach, thought and other personal factors, behavior, and the environment all operate as interacting determinants. Because of the reciprocal causation, therapeutic efforts can be directed at all three determinants. Psychosocial functioning is improved by altering faulty thought patterns, by increasing behavioral competencies and skills in dealing with situational demands, and by altering adverse social conditions. In fact, you achieve the most powerful effect by altering each of these sources of reciprocal causation.

efficacy as they were undergoing these powerful mastery experiences.

EVANS: Has this early experience that you've just related led you to develop the background and the research which in turn led to your interest in self-efficacy?

BANDURA: Yes. We were getting very good maintenance of change and good transfer in that the people were able to resume the activities in their life that they had avoided before. We felt that we could expand the transfer benefits even further by adding a program of self-directed mastery after they had overcome the phobia. By succeeding on their own, they would not attribute their success to the mastery aids or to the therapist. We created experiences for them where they coped with a phobic object on their own. This provided a dramatic demonstration that we had restored their coping capabilities, rather than they were able to function more effectively because we were present to aid them and protect them.

It was in this research project that people were coming in and telling us how they were changing other areas of their life in very positive ways. I decided to develop a methodology to measure changes in people's beliefs in their coping capabilities. We found that we could predict with considerable accuracy the speed of therapeutic change and the degree of generality from the extent which their perceived efficacy was enhanced. It was in that context that I began my research on self-efficacy as a basic cognitive mechanism governing human functioning.

EVANS: That makes the transition from your earlier work to your interest in self-efficacy and the process of this transition particularly interesting because you were exploring a construct empirically before examining it more rigorously within an experimental framework.

BANDURA: That's right.

EVANS: This seems to be the course of development of most of your contributions—moving from sophisticated empirical observation to more rigorous experimental validation. Now, also

The third approach, cognitive behavior therapy, overlaps a fair amount with the social cognitive approach. However, cognitive behavior therapists focus mainly on changing faulty thought patterns on the assumption that most behavior problems arise from faulty thought. To alter how people behave one must alter how they think. So there are three quite different approaches, all of which tend to be categorized by the general public as behavior modification.

EVANS: Hans Eysenck, who is a bitter, bitter critic of psychoanalysis and who claims title to the term "behavior therapy," talked a little bit in the dialogue I completed with him about a typical problem that one would encounter in therapy—the problem of symptom substitution. He was challenging the essentially psychodynamic assumption that if you remove a symptom—say, a neurotic self-destructive symptom—eventually another symptom even more destructive could appear. He was disputing the assumption that symptom removal is not going to solve any problem at all unless this includes some considerable insight. Eysenck contends there isn't any good empirical evidence of this contention of the psychoanalysts. He has observed that you can simply remove that symptom and the person can function perfectly well. These are what he considered to be "asinine" reports by individuals like Lewis Wolberg, the psychoanalyst, who specialized in the use of hypnosis. Wolberg had, as a patient, a trumpet player who had developed some sort of paralysis of muscles in the mouth and could no longer play the trumpet. So Wolberg, through hypnotic suggestion, created a slight twitch in the man's arm as a substitute symptom. This man could once again play the trumpet. Wolberg then proceeded on a course of psychoanalytic treatment which would provide the patient the necessary "emotional insight." Eysenck contends that this kind of observation is based on an assumption that is simplistic and misleading.

Of course, as Eysenck suggests, behavior therapists are often attempting to modify such self-destructive "symptoms." Now, you, yourself, have been interested in phobias. Psychoanalysts might regard phobias as symptoms of more profound dimensions. Do you want to remove that phobia without regard to providing "emotional insight" for the patient? The psychoanalyst might claim that the phobia may have a utility to the individual. If you remove that phobia without fully understanding the whole psychodynamic process, another symptom may occur that is even possibly more destructive. Starting with that assumption, how would the social cognitive therapist look at this same problem?

BANDURA: Well, first of all, I would not regard a phobia as a symptom because that's buying into the pseudo-disease model of divergent behavior as diseased behavior.

EVANS: OK. That's very important to bring out.

BANDURA: Certainly a dysfunction has a history. Consider a case in which, let us say, a child in school does not know how to read and encounters a lot of academic problems. Undoubtedly there have been many aversive experiences in the child's history. One does not have to analyze the whole dismal history in order to help the child acquire an academic skill that would give the child mastery over the subject matter. In the case of phobias, we have treated hundreds of them with the mastery modeling treatment with uniform success. These people have experienced 10, 15, 20, or 30 years in which their lives had been incapacitated by their phobic dread. Originally I thought this a trivial problem, but it turned out that for the people who sought treatment, their lives were greatly impaired. They could not go hiking, camping or walking through open fields. Their occupational activity was adversely affected. We treated plumbers who could not work under houses, geologists who were terrified of field work, firefighters who could not fight grass fires, telephone repairmen who were terrified of getting to the poles because they believed snakes were lurking around the poles, and so on. During the summer they were

plagued by ruminations about reptiles. They could not visit friends in rustic areas. They experienced recurrent nightmares, so they suffered major impairments of functioning. Within a few hours of guided mastery treatment, we were able to eliminate the phobias in everyone. Rather than finding symptom substitution, if anything, we found positive changes in other areas of functioning.

Results of tests for the effects of the treatment sparked my interest in the notion of perceived self-efficacy. Quite apart from changing the phobic behavior, the mastery experiences eliminated nightmares and aversive dreams. This is a profound generalized effect in which waking mastery experiences modify dream activity.

EVANS: Certainly a dramatic improvement for the patient wasn't it?

BANDURA: For most people this was a dramatic personal change. Here they were plagued with this problem for 10, 20, or 30 years and they were able to overcome it in a few hours. Many of them described their experience as follows: life had been distressed, handicapped and constrained by phobia for a long period. They originally believed that personality patterns were so fixed that it would be very difficult change them. As they mastered their phobia they began to say "If I can change this area of my life, surely there must be areas in which I can be more venturesome." They were coming in and reporting that they had been putting themselves to the test and improving their public speaking, social life and the like. There would be no reason to expect such generalized benefits if only behavior was being altered. It was evident that we were doing something much more fundamental than just removing a phobia. We were altering personal beliefs about their coping efficacy which they were then putting to the test, succeeding and initiating positive changes in other areas of their lives. It was at that point that I decided to measure what was happening to people's sense of

in terms of this social cognitive approach to behavior modification, you mentioned that part of the repertoire of strategies you were including was the use of modeling. We've talked earlier about Miller and Dollard's book, *Social Learning and Imitation* (1941) and you mentioned that you had read this book in 1941 and were quite intrigued with it.

BANDURA: In my early research I examined the social transmission of aggression through modeling. This got me into the social controversies of the effects of televised violence on children.

EVANS: Of course, here you were entering the arena of influencing public policy.

BANDURA: People were questioned whether televised modeling could possibly have any effect on children.

EVANS: Now, this is very early.

BANDURA: Yes. The modification of fears and phobic disorders could be used to demonstrate the power of modeling. Some of our early research was conducted with children who suffered from dog phobias. Their phobic behavior was reduced or eliminated by having them observe peer models engage in the feared activities without any untoward effect.

EVANS: So in a way the logic of this was that you would use a therapeutic mode to demonstrate modeling.

BANDURA: Yes. I could demonstrate the power of modeling for therapeutic purposes. At that time I was working mainly with modeling alone. As you know, one's work is greatly enriched by graduate students. As graduate students, Bruni Ritter and Ed Blanchard were helping me with that research. Bruni suggested that we add a performance component to it. This greatly increased the power of the treatment. We began to add other mastery aids and evolved a uniformly powerful treatment. Subsequent research indicated that guided mastery modeling reduces anxiety and enhances coping behavior through the efficacy mechanism. We began to develop a theory on how to enhance perceived self-efficacy. The theory and research have now been expanded to diverse domains. We are gaining a better understanding of how self-belief affects thought, motivation and behavior.

I've come to the conclusion that the treatments that are most effective are built on an empowerment model. If you really want to help people, you provide them with the competencies, build a strong self-belief, and create opportunities for them to exercise those competencies. Consider the models of change that have proven successful. Our guided mastery treatment of phobia dysfunction is based on an empowerment model. We empower people with the coping skills and a strong sense of coping efficacy. At the familial level, Jerry Patterson's treatment of hyperaggressive children is based on a familial empowerment model. You empower parents with more effective ways of relating to their children and coping with interpersonal problems. Families change for the better not by sitting around and talking about problems, but by providing parents with the kind of skills and understanding they need to deal effectively with their children and each other.

EVANS: You're providing a repertoire of skills that they can now apply.

BANDURA: Yes. You model the skills for them and assist them in their efforts to make desired changes in the family. The empowerment model also applies at the educational level. I am presently involved in a MacArthur Foundation group, seeking to gain a better understanding of how children in a high-risk environment ever make it out of dismal environments and of how those environments could be changed so more children make it. Jim Comer (1980) has been developing an educational restructuring model which focuses not on changing the curriculum or teaching methods, but on raising expectations and motivation for learning. He has developed a collaborative educational model to achieve this. Parents, teacher representatives, the principal and psychological school personnel form a collaborative governance group that restructures the school environment. This governance group establishes priorities, mobilizes available resources, sets academic standards and conveys expectations of achievement. Parents have an increased sense of responsibility for and control over the quality of educational life of their children. Parents play an active role in the educational change. They assess what resources are needed and they find ways of getting them. Parents are actively involved in the tutoring of children. Parents develop and carry out social programs. This approach empowers the very people whose lives are strongly affected by providing them with a creative mechanism whereby they can exercise influence in areas of their life over which they can command some influence. Comer has achieved success in transforming ghetto schools into schools for educational achievement rather than schools for failure. If you create motivational conditions for learning, raise children's sense of intellectual efficacy, provide them with educational support and guidance and create academic norms and standards to which children can aspire, they will become good learners. This type of educational restructuring is built on an empowerment model.

2

Aggression and
Violence

In this section, Dr. Bandura and I discuss the development of his theories and research in the area of aggression including the classic Bobo Doll experiment, in which his concept of modeling was incorporated into a study of aggressive behavior in children. We also discuss how results from research in this field have become an issue in public policy regarding such issues as the role of mass media in generating violence. He presents examples of how reports in the media serve as models of violent or aggressive behavior. Dr. Bandura then discusses his view of how the problem of censorship in controlling depiction of violence in the media can be reconciled with the need to somehow modify the depiction of violence in the media.

EVANS: To begin this section of our discussion, Dr. Bandura, I simply have to ask you to discuss your classic laboratory study dealing with modeling of aggression employing the Bobo doll, otherwise our readers would never forgive me. How did you first become interested in laboratory studies on aggression?·

BANDURA: I first became interested in laboratory studies of modeling of aggression when Dick Walters and I conducted a large study on the familial antecedents of hyperaggressive delinquents. We were interested, not in why a youngster who comes from a broken home, who has tremendous difficulty in school, who resides in a high-delinquency area, and whose parents engage in criminal activities, might develop an aggressive style of behavior. The more challenging question is how do children survive high-risk environments and develop prosocial styles and behavior under such adverse social conditions.

EVANS: In other words, to say that you were just looking specifically at this behavior is probably rather misleading, is that correct?

BANDURA: Yes. We were trying to explain how children from advantaged backgrounds develop serious antisocial patterns of behavior. We were interested in explaining why a youngster who is of average or brighter intelligence, who comes from an intact home, who lives in a non-delinquency area, develops a hyperaggressive behavior. We found that one factor that contributed to aggression was extensive parental modeling of hostility and aggressive behavior. The parents were nonpermissive and punitive for aggression in the home, but demanded, encouraged and supported aggressiveness outside the home. They would side with the youngster in aggression toward peers and teachers. We were struck by the influence parental modeling had in the development of aggression. I decided that there should be some way of studying this process experimentally. We adopted the Bobo doll paradigm to study the extent to which young children might be adopting aggressive patterns of behavior through modeling. Dorrie and Sheila Ross helped me with this research. We modeled very unique forms of aggression that they would not have learned elsewhere. It was in that context that we began the series of laboratory studies on the factors governing the extent to which modeled aggression will be adopted. As you know, one can discover fruitful leads if one is sensitive to research findings. For example, there was this one child who had watched the modeled aggression on film. In the experimental room, where the children were tested for how much aggression they would show spontaneously, he displayed very little aggression. When I was walking back to the nursery school with him, he said, "You know, I saw a cartoon with Rocky, and Rocky sat on the Bobo doll and he punched it in the nose." He ran off the entire aggressive repertoire, not only the whole repertoire of physical aggression, but all the verbal aggression as well. What a striking demonstration of the difference between learning and performance! This youngster had learned the entire aggressive repertoire, had shown very little spontaneously, but was able to reenact the entire repertoire. I could have written the entire script from what he described.

EVANS: Instead of assuming that you have to look at this through some kind of biological paradigm or through some paradigm that generated, say, aggression through frustration, you were now looking at modeling as being a very important factor at the acquisition end.

BANDURA: Yes. A theory of aggression must explain three aspects: First, how aggressive patterns of behavior are developed; second, what provokes people to behave aggressively; and third, what determines whether they are going to continue to resort to an aggressive behavior pattern on future occasions.

EVANS: Looking at this as a social psychologist, I think that your model of research generated an entirely new way of investigating aggression. The Bobo doll experiment, of course, generated a number of similar types of studies and ultimately had quite a bit of impact on the thinking of even the Presidential Commission on Violence in the Media.

BANDURA: When I'm introduced at invited lectures at other universities, the students place a Bobo doll by the lectern. From time to time I have been asked to autograph one. The Bobo doll has achieved stardom in psychological circles.

EVANS: Now perhaps we can discuss some of the implications in this work as it began to be replicated and expanded. Over time it began to be looked at in terms of how the media in general might trigger more aggression in our society.

BANDURA: One reason this research generated considerable interest is because the prevailing view at that time was that exposure to aggression had cathartic effects. Namely, it drained an aggressive drive which reduces the likelihood of aggression. Our research showed that in fact, exposure to aggressive models tended to increase aggression. These findings had interesting social implications.

EVANS: Now, of course, in terms of the broader implications and applications of your studies and thoughts about symbolic modeling in the media, clearly this began to draw attention from public policy makers. In fact, as a number of investigators began replicating your work, doing similar studies, the collective impact of your work began to draw attention from members of Congress who were becoming concerned about such possibly aversive effects of the entertainment media.

BANDURA: Yes, I became a frequent commuter to congressional hearings.

EVANS: Are we somehow, through our entertainment media (even in news presentations) demonstrating what you found experimentally? It was being argued that perhaps many of the increasingly violent aggressive acts in society, increases in crime, assaults and so on, may be directly related to this high degree of modeling of aggression in the media.

BANDURA: Most people would minimize the effect of televised violence in the abstract, but readily acknowledge it when it can jeopardize their personal safety. If you were to ask airline pilots whether or not modeled aggression affects aggressive patterns of behavior, most would probably question or minimize its effects. But if you ask them whether modeling an aggressive style of behavior involving airliners can have hazardous effects, they would express a very different view. Sometimes the television networks perform excellent experiments that unintentionally reveal significant modeling effects. This is graphically illustrated in the televised program "The Doomsday Flight." It involved a scenario in which an extortionist calls the airline and announces that he had placed an altitude-sensitive bomb on a transcontinental flight. He tries to extort money from the airline by claiming that when the airline descends below 5,000 feet, the altitude-sensitive bomb will explode. In the plot he is outwitted. The airline reroutes the plane to an airport above 5,000 feet. When this program was shown on television, I wrote to the FAA (Federal Aviation Association) for data on the frequency of extortion threats for months preceding that of the program, and the extortion threats after this scenario was televised. Extortion threats must be reported to the FAA by requirements of law. There was a substantial increase in the number of extortion threats immediately after the program had been televised. But even more informative was the incidence of modeling after this program was included in a package of reruns. The airline association tried to get this thing off the air because it was creating major problems. When this program was televised in different cities, it was not unusual for an extortion plot to be called in the next day. When televised in Fairbanks, Alaska, an extortionist called in with the same plot and collected $25,000 from Western Airlines in a flight leaving for Hawaii. When it was shown in San Francisco, the plot was called in, but the extortionist was apprehended during the money drop from a helicopter. When it was shown in Sydney, Australia, an extortionist actually built an altitude-sensitive bomb, put it in an airport locker, and directed the airline personnel to it to demonstrate that he knew how to build one. He claimed that he had placed a similar altitude-sensitive bomb on a Qantas Airline flight to Hong Kong. He collected $560,000 from the airline. They discovered there was no bomb. As far as the airlines were concerned, there was no doubt in their mind that television can influence behavior and they had the large cash drain to substantiate it. The temporal patterning of modeling provided convincing data.

In this particular form of aggression the pattern of behavior required no special apparatus. It did not require the aggressor to be present. It did not require any physical ingenuity. The network provided the extortion strategy. These conditions facilitate modeling.

EVANS: Is the situation involving the extortionist in Montreal an example of this?

BANDURA: Yes. The rerun was shown on Montreal television. The next day the extortionist used the bomb plot, including the 5,000-foot sensitive altitude in an effort to extract a quarter of a million dollars from British Overseas Airways. By now the airlines had become so familiar with this oft-repeated scenario that they rerouted that flight and landed it in Denver, which is 5,300 feet. This is cutting it quite close. I'm sure that the passengers who ended up in Denver rather than London, had strong feelings about the possible power of televised modeling. A TWA flight, bound from Madrid for New York, was similarly rerouted when a Madrid viewer called in the bomb hoax after seeing it in a television rerun. A rerun in Paris produced the same extortion scenario.

EVANS: I was thinking of some of your observations with respect to an experience I had on a television program in Houston. At that time I was involved in producing and moderating a panel series of television shows on delinquency. On one show we discussed the kinds of modeling that influenced the three delinquents appearing on the show to commit some of their crimes. On the television program with me were program directors of three local commercial television stations and some television producers. The TV producers and directors were saying that there's no way that these so-called delinquents were going to relate their delinquency to television. Television just simply cannot affect criminal behavior, that's just too ridiculous. They were perfectly happy to have me ask these kids about this right there in front of the cameras. I asked them if they thought television influenced them to commit crimes. One of these teenagers asked, "What do you mean by that?" I said, "Well, you've been arrested, you're incarcerated now for stealing cars, did what you ever saw on TV influence you to steal cars?" These teenagers actually described a television show, one of these situations in a police story where they were showing viewers how to jump-start a car. These kids said, "This is how we learned to do this."

BANDURA: This illustrates how interesting data on this issue can be obtained quite directly. Sometimes the research that costs little reveals a lot. There is a fascinating report of a survey study conducted by a psychologist who was an inmate in a maximum security prison. He found that the inmates improved their criminal skills by watching crime programs. They learned better burglary techniques, how to hotwire cars, and how to pull off bunco fraud. They learned how police work in catching offenders and how alarm systems operate. They are brought up-to-date on new police procedures. The inmates then copied entire criminal strategies. This is an interesting document because the incidents of modeled criminality were verified against police records. For prison inmates, crime shows are educational television. Many take notes while watching. In producing the programs, producers want to be as authentic as possible, so they display the newest techniques. If viewers act on incomplete information, their attempts may prove unsuccessful. One youngster learned from a television program how to break into telephone coin boxes. But what the program did not tell him is that Ma Bell has a silent alarm system built into pay phones so when he broke into the coin box he was apprehended.

There was one program in which a prison escapee breaches a police barricade by rushing to a hospital and getting into an ambulance. As the ambulance passes through the blockade with its siren screaming, he escaped. An inmate used the same plot when he escaped from prison. He rushed to a hospital emergency room that was nearby and screamed that his brother was pinned under a car. The ambulance driver told him to jump into the ambulance. He was waved through a police barricade with sirens blaring.

An important question concerns conditions under which televised modeling is likely to have an effect, since obviously not everyone acts on what they have seen. One needs a theory that can now explain under what conditions are people going to act on the knowledge they have acquired. Here, of course, I draw the important distinction between the power of the media to produce learning and its power to affect action. The learning effects are rather uniform. If children watch one hundred ways of killing people hundreds of times they will learn one hundred ways to kill people. But the effects on action are variable. We need to explain the conditions under which people are going to act on what they have learned. Aggression is more functional for some people than for others.

EVANS: You earlier referred to pro-social behavior. We are obviously recognizing where the media can model socially destructive behaviors. Of course, the media present models of other behaviors, as well.

BANDURA: A number of experiments have been reported showing that if pro-social behavior is modeled it increases pro-social tendencies in children. So television can have a pro-social impact. It is unfortunate that televised modeling is not used more to cultivate the positive potentialities of people.

EVANS: Now, another aspect of this thing is that a lot of phrases are created by the media referring to destructive modeling. I'm referring particularly to phrases like "copycat killer." Essentially, what law enforcement people seem to be suggesting is that these criminals copy other criminals' modus operandi and that this generates another series of crimes of the same sort.

BANDURA: Your question raises the issue of how events are reported. Are broadcasters spreading what they are reporting?

EVANS: Can you give an example of this?

BANDURA: The most striking example is airline hijacking. The first airline hijacking occurred in Hungary during the Hungarian uprising. The next hijackings were Cubans hijacking planes to Miami. Then the Americans picked it up and, within a year, there was a wave of airline hijackings. This strategy rapidly diffused internationally so before long seventy different countries had experienced airline hijackings. When Cubans were hijacking to Miami, they were hailed as heroes, but when Americans were hijacking to Havana, they were regarded as mentally deranged. The diagnosis of psychopathology depended very heavily on the direction of the unscheduled flight. The hijacking strategy diffused not only within the United States but spread very rapidly internationally.

Like most diffusion phenomena, it is started by a striking example. It spreads rapidly in a contagious fashion. After it has been widely adopted, it is decreased by informal countermeasures. Airlines began to develop behavioral profiles that identified likely hijackers. Because of international agreements, hijackers could not find any place to land commandeered planes. As this phenomenon began to wane, there was one counterexample in the United States that produced a sudden rise in hijackings. It was based on a novel scenario that D. B. Cooper modeled. He traded passengers for a parachute and a large bundle of money and then parachuted out of the plane. He obviously knew a lot about airplanes because this type of strategy can work with a 727 which has an exit out of the tail, otherwise the parachute would get strung up in the stabilizers or tail. A lot of time and money was spent trying to find Cooper or the bundle of money to demonstrate publicly that the strategy did not work.

I wrote to the FAA to determine how many people were modeling the parachute extortion strategy, which had never been used before. Within a few months there were 18 incidents of direct modeling of parachute extortion strategy. The first person who imitated the Cooper strategy parachuted over Colorado. The Air Force planted an electronic signal in the parachute so as he fluttered down, there was a reception committee waiting to meet him. The Air Force announced that this should be a lesson to everyone. It was. The next hijacker brought his own parachute aboard and tossed out the bugged parachute while in flight. This sent the pursuit planes chasing the bugged parachute, as the extortionist landed safely on the sweeping plains of Utah. He later got caught when he boasted about his success to a person sitting next to him at the bar, who happened to be an off-duty policeman. The third parachuter decided that he could increase the chances of success by parachuting over the Honduras jungle where pursuit planes have difficulty landing. He escaped safely with a large bundle of money. The international hijackers then added the extortion component, so they demanded money on their flights to Libya or to Cuba. The first time they tried this, the money courier was an FBI agent who overpowered the hijackers. The next hijackers then revised the scenario by demanding that the money courier be nude. The public display of nudity did not improve the already-tarnished image of the FBI. This example illustrates how counterstrategies can produce innovations and creativity in transgressive behavior to increase its chances of success. It is very difficult to get rid of transgressive behavior after it has been planted in people's consciousness and it carries high prospect of money. Transgressors can always figure ways of revising it slightly to increase its safety. After a while people were hijacking airplanes who did not even know what to do with parachutes. The airlines finally solved the problem by announcing publicly that the exit door was sealed from the outside so it could not be opened from the inside. That solved the proplem of the continued social diffusion of that strategy.

EVANS: Assuming that these destructive models are around in the media, what could be done to try to contol this type of aggressive modeling that can lead to some of these destructive behaviors? Of course, we have the problem of being concerned about censorship.

BANDURA: When I was writing the 1973 aggression book, *Aggression: A Social Learning Analysis* (Bandura, 1973), I considered three different approaches to reducing gratuitous use of violence for commercial purposes. One is the congressional route. The public puts pressure on Congress to try to place some limits on the use of gratuitous violence in television programming. This is an ineffectual mechanism because television content is protected by the First Amendment and no one would want to give Congress the power to police what people can see on television. After attending a number of congressional hearings, to which I referred earlier in our dialogue, I realized that these hearings were not producing results. They were taking on the character of television reruns.

EVANS: So you're saying these congressional hearings were just politically motivated?

BANDURA: A congressional committee calls the networks to task for gratuitous use of violence. They produce a testimony to that effect and subpoena records showing instances where there was deliberate use of violence that was not contributing to the plot, but was presumably designed to hold viewers' attention. Researchers testify on the possible effects of exposure to televised violence. Network researchers dispute the evidence, much like the tobacco industry disputes any evidence of a causal relation between smoking and cancer or other health problems. The congressional members make ominous threats that they will take action if the networks do not clean up their act. The congressional threat gains public support for the networks by arousing fear of governmental censorship. In fact, Congress does not have any power to control program content, nor would the public want to grant them that power. So this scenario is repeated from time to time with the same cast of participants and the same lack of results.

The second strategy is to use the networks' own system of self-regulation. This approach turns out to be equally ineffective because program content is strongly determined by marketing pressures. What people are shown is largely dictated by what will deliver the largest audience to advertisers. There is a common misbelief that violence is prevalent because it is highly attractive to people. The empirical evidence disputes this view. There is no correlation between the amount of violence in programs and Nielsen popularity ratings. Deleting violence from programs does not change the attraction ratings. If you examine the top-ten programs year after year, programs that dwell heavily on violence rarely make it in the top 10. People are attracted more to variety shows and comedies.

This raises the question of what function violence serves in programming? It is used not because it attracts viewers. In fact, networks have to sanitize it so it does not turn people away. Violence is prevalent because of program constraints and production costs. People are attracted to conflict. If you have only twenty-five minutes for a dramatic production, there is little time for psychological subtleties or plot development. The easiest way to present conflict is through physical violence and the easiest way to resolve it before the last commercial is to knock of the antagonist. So program constraints create pressure to use physical violence to depict conflict.

Another problem that networks have with viewers is that they do not sit glued to the television set. They wander in and out, and often do something else simultaneously. So networks have to figure out some way to grab and hold viewers' attention. Talking heads are not a very effective way of doing it. So networks use a lot of action and high decibels to command attention. Physical action becomes an effective attention device.

In order to portray conflict in a way that would hold attention requires talented writers. Not many talented writers want to be turning out television scenarios over and over again. So there is a limited talent pool for creating engrossing drama. What gets shown on television is largely determined by production costs per thousand viewers. Good programming that incurs high production costs is not profitable. Furthermore, as a series becomes popular, annual raises drive up the costs. It's not all that unusual for a program to get killed off when it's very popular simply because it is no longer financially profitable. The answer to the prevalence of the violent format lies more in production costs, program time constraints, limited talent pool, and the need for a vehicle to grab and hold attention than in viewers' cravings for violence. Viewers often get blamed for the prevalence of televised violence, and networks use democracy arguments for why they should not be deprived of it.

The third, and most effective, approach to the improvement of television relies on the power of positive example. Greater progress is achieved by rewarding constructive practices than by curtailing objectionable ones. Programs that make gratuitous use of violence can be put out of business by providing people with more interesting alternatives. The power of constructive alternatives is nowhere better illustrated than in children's programming, which has aroused the greatest public concern. For years parents complained about the commercial fare served their children without achieving any improvements in children's programming. The appearance of children's programs on public television, such as Sesame Street, demonstrated that programs that are instructive, as well as entertaining, can attract large children's audiences. A viable public broadcasting system, free of commercial pressures, is perhaps the best means of improving and diversifying television offerings.

EVANS: Moving now to a more generic aspect of aggression, how do you feel about the sociobiologist's view of aggression? As you know, they postulated an essentially genetically programmed view of aggression.

BANDURA: Sociobiology relies heavily on neurophysiological and Darwinian selection mechanisms. It is true that over the years we have evolved biological systems that serve basic functions. So one can find some commonalities in basic biological mechanisms. But the evidence that impresses me more is the tremendous cultural diversity. People have a remarkable capacity to adapt to markedly different environmental conditions. They display markedly different patterns of behavior, tastes, and preferences. Another problem with sociobiology is that social change can occur very rapidly, whereas the Darwinian genetic conveyance moves at a snail's pace. Rapid social changes create explanatory problems for sociobiological theories.

EVANS: So plasticity appears to be an important characteristic of human nature?

BANDURA: The most striking human characteristic is plasticity. It is the distinctively universal feature of human nature.

EVANS: You are suggesting that instead of accepting that perhaps we are genetically programmed for something as specific as aggressive responses, perhaps even more generically the human organism may be genetically programmed for a much broader coping capacity, plasticity?

BANDURA: That's right. Plasticity does not mean that we do not have a human nature. Plasticity is the distinctive feature of human nature. It is because we have evolved neural systems with which to code, retain, and process information that we are capable of these distinctive human characteristics.

EVANS: From a social cognitive perspective, what do you see as these characteristics?

BANDURA: One distinctive attribute is our tremendous capacity for symbolization. Symbol systems provide the vehicle for thought. By representing their experiences symbolically, people can give meaning and continuity to their lives. Through symbol systems, they can communicate across time and space.

A second distinctive human attribute is our forethought capability. Because people can project into the future, they can regulate and motivate themselves by anticipated outcomes and aspirations. They anticipate likely consequences of possible actions, set goals for themselves, and otherwise plan courses of action that lead to valued futures. It is the capacity to extrapolate future consequences that increases the prospects of human survival. If humans were ruled solely by immediate consequences they would have destroyed more of the ecological supports of life. Forethought often saves us from the perils of a foreshortened perspective.

The third basic human attribute is our advanced vicarious learning capacity. As I noted previously, people have a capacity to acquire patterns of behavior, attitudes, and emotional proclivities through observation without having to go through the tedious trial-and-error process.

Another distinctive human attribute is our self-regulatory capabilities. People are not only reactors to external events. They are self-reactors with some capacity for self-directedness and self-evaluation. Self-regulatory capabilities enable people to exercise some control over their own motivation and actions. A further distinctive human characteristic is the capacity for self-reflection. People can reflect on their own experiences, they can think about their own thought processes and behavior. They can act on their ideas or predict occurrences from them, judge from the results the adequacy of their thoughts and change them accordingly.

From the sociobiology point of view, genetics and other biological factors play a central role in aggression because aggressive fighters contribute to the gene pool and the weaklings are being squeezed out of the gene pool. It is true that people have evolved neurophysiological mechanisms that mediate aggression. But that is not where aggression originates.

EVANS: But among human organisms the weaklings aren't always eliminated from the gene pool. In fact, under some circumstances genetically inferior individuals may survive. How does this apply?

BANDURA: In humans the use of weapons, the power of organized members and social sanctions have greatly reduced the relation between physical build and aggressiveness. A gang of weaklings can beat up a tough opponent. A puny person with a gun can wipe out a powerfully built opponent. Social sanctions also reduce the relation between build—which is affected by hormones and genes—and aggression. The evolutionary consequences of aggression vary across species. If you house a dominant male mouse, and a subordinate male with a female mouse, the dominant male will produce 86 percent of the offspring. But in humans, reproduction rates and partnerships are determined more by looks, money, religious beliefs, and birth control practices. Social factors heavily influence human male selection and reproduction rates. Social sanctions prohibit brawny males from going around impregnating whomever they desire.

EVANS: So you see sociobiologists as overstating the importance of neurophysiological mechanisms in aggression?

BANDURA: Neurophysiological mechanisms mediate aggression. But these mechanisms are under social influence and cognitive control. If I am insulted but it goes unrecognized, I will have a quiescent hypothalamus. If I go around reading hostile intent all around me, I will have a very busy hypothalamus. Social factors determine the form that aggression takes, where and when it will be expressed and who is selected as targets. Research by Delgado (1967) illustrates how social learning factors regulate animals' responses when the same neural structure is stimulated. Delgado studied a colony of monkeys who had brain implants. He could stimulate their hypothalamus by radio transmission. This was a colony of monkeys in which they had an established dominance hierarchy.

When Delgado stimulated the hypothalamus of the boss monkey, he beat up the subordinate male, but he did not beat up the females, with whom he was on very good terms. So there was a good deal of selection in his choice of targets. When a monkey who occupied the lowest rank in the power structure was hypothalamically stimulated at the same neural site, she began to cower and showed increased submissiveness. Delgado then changed the power hierarchy by introducing more submissive members into the group, at which point this formerly submissive monkey now beat up those who were lower in rank when stimulated. Stimulating the same neural site activated aggression when a monkey occupied a high-power rank, but activated cowering and submission in a monkey who occupied a low rank. This is a striking illustration of how activating the same neural site can produce radically different behavior depending on level of social power.

In large-scale inhumanities, people are driven to violence by their ideologies, not their biologies. There is tremendous cross-cultural variation in levels of aggressiveness. In societies where aggression is devalued, it is rarely modeled and it serves no functional value—people live peaceably. In societies where aggression is widely modeled, it is a mode of behavior for gaining status, power and social approval, and it brings material benefits; people threaten, maim, and kill each other. It is also interesting to note that the changes in aggression occur over time within societies. At one time the Swiss were the main suppliers of military mercenaries. The Swiss have not been assaulting others for several generations.

EVANS: The American Indians are a good example of this, aren't they?

BANDURA: The early American Indian tribes varied tremendously in aggressiveness. There were the fighting tribes, such as the Apache and Comanche, and pacific tribes, such as the Zuni and Hopi. In contemporary life in America, devout Quakers and Hutterites do not go around mugging people. The substantial variation in aggressive patterns of behavior both within and across societies is testimony to the powerful influence of social and cognitive mechanisms of control.

EVANS: Would you talk a little about the instigators of aggression?

BANDURA: There are two broad classes of motivators or instigators of aggressive behavior. The first set of motivators are aversive conditions. This is often called frustration. What people call frustration includes different distressing experiences. Stressors produce emotional arousal rather than a distinct aggressive drive that needs to be discharged. Emotional arousal can activate all kinds of responses. When stressed or frustrated, some people become dependent and seek help. Others show withdrawal and resignation. Some aggress. Others may respond with psychosomatic reactions. Still others anaesthetize themselves against a miserable reality with drugs or alcohol. But most people increase constructive efforts to overcome the obstacles and problems that are frustrating them.

EVANS: What determines which reaction will be followed?

BANDURA: Which mode of reaction is developed and preferred depends on what one has learned as a way of coping with the problems and how well it has worked.

EVANS: Now, to describe further these aversive instigators of aggression . . .

BANDURA: The aversive instigators represent the push to aggression. People do not have to be emotionally aroused to aggress. Much aggression is performed because of expected benefits. So in examining the motivators for aggression, we need to consider not only the push of distress, but the pull of expected rewards for successful aggression.

This leads to the third component of the social cognitive theory of aggression, namely, what determines whether people will continue to resort to aggression. In the theory that I have been proposing, aggression serves multiple purposes. Some people will resort to aggression to get material benefits. Others behave aggressively because it gains them status and social approval. Still others rely on aggressive conquests to build their self-esteem and sense of manliness. Some people derive satisfaction from seeing pain inflicted on those they hate. And in many instances, people resort to aggression to terminate mistreatment. So aggression can serve multiple purposes. This summarizes the general structure of the social cognitive model of aggression.

3

Moral Development and Moral Disengagement

In this section, Dr. Bandura and I discuss his conceptions of moral development and moral disengagement. We discuss the process through which individuals may "conveniently" engage in acts which are diametrically opposed to their avowed moral principles. Dr. Bandura and I discuss his notions of the process of moral disengagement with illustrations such as how victims of atrocities are often dehumanized in order to morally justify such atrocities and how the use of nuclear weapons might even be justified in this process.

EVANS: Related to our discussion of your work in aggression and modeling is the way the individual chooses to respond to a model of a destructive act. This introduces the very critical question of morality in the individual. It becomes a very important set of questions because clearly, philosophers, theologians, Piaget, Freud, and on and on, have all considered morality and moral development. It would be interesting to see how you began to approach morality and moral development.

BANDURA: Much of our theorizing and research has been concerned with how to instill morality in people. I have been interested in the way in which moral standards are internalized and regulate human conduct. In social cognitive theory, morality is governed by self-regulatory mechanisms. People adopt standards and then act in line with those standards. They engage in behavior that gives them a sense of self-respect and self-worth and refrain from behavior that leads to self-censure. Indeed, the most devastating self-punishment is self-contempt. Most theories approach the issue of morality in terms of inner standards, conscience, and super ego, as though they function as a set of fixed regulators of moral conduct.

EVANS: This led to your thinking concerning moral disengagement, did it not?

BANDURA: Yes. People have a capacity to selectively engage or disengage their morality from inhumane conduct. This permits radically different behavior with the same moral principles. I have been studying eight psychological mechanisms of moral disengagement. The issue of moral disengagement has tremendous theoretical and social import because most of the wide-scale inhumanities are performed by otherwise considerate and compassionate people. It requires social conditions conducive to inhumane behavior rather than monstrous people to produce heinous deeds.

In developing a conceptual model of the mechanisms of moral disengagement, I have identified several points in a behavioral process where the disengagement can occur. The first point is at the level of reconstruing the behavior itself by moral justification. People ordinarily do not engage in detrimental conduct until they have justified to themselves the morality of their cause. In this mechanism, destructive behavior is redefined as serving moral purposes. People then act on a moral imperative. Over the years, a tremendous amount of human violence has been performed in the name of religious principles, righteous ideologies and nationalistic imperatives. This is violence performed in the service of ideology or principle. Military situations provide striking examples of moral disengagement. People are socialized not to kill. Socialized people are converted into skilled fighters not by changing their personality, motives, or moral standards. Rather this is accomplished by redefining the morality of killing. By providing a just cause for killing, a killing becomes morally acceptable and can be done free from self-censuring reactions. A striking example is Sgt. York, who is one of the outstanding fighters in the history of modern warfare. He was a conscientious objector. He refused to serve in the forces. One of the commanders on the base called him in and quoted him chapter and verse from the Bible that he can serve both God and country by becoming a fighter. York spent a marathon weekend in prayer at the foot of a mountain and persuaded himself that, indeed, he can serve both God and country by becoming a fighter. He became a highly decorated one. Currently, a lot of holy terror is being perpetrated in the name of religious principles, in the Mideast, and in Northern Ireland, and other places.

Another disengagement mechanism is advantageous comparison. Behavior takes on its meaning from what it's compared against. If you create advantageous comparisons, you can transform an otherwise destructive behavior into appearing benign or even altruistic. This is why it is very difficult to argue on moral grounds that one should not resort to violence to produce social change. Those who use violence for social change point to the fact that the democracies of the United States, France, and England were born of violence. This type of justi-

of morality. One of these is dehumanization. If you analyze how enemies are depicted over many wars, they are always portrayed in dehumanized, and bestial terms. If you look at the reports of, let's say the Greek torturers, they referred to their victims as "worms." Primo Levi cites a striking incident that occurred in a Nazi death camp where he was interned. Someone asked the commandant, why they went to such great lengths to degrade people when they were going to kill them anyway? He replied that you have to degrade them to the point of subhuman objects because those who operated the gas chambers would be less distressed. Dehumanization was not just sadism, but a calculated policy of moral disengagement to enable others to perform the gruesome mass killings. People are dehumanized by calling them "gooks" or "pigs." If dehumanization does not remove moral restraints, bestial qualities are attributed to them. It's much easier to behave inhumanely towards someone who is subhuman or bestial than it is to someone who is humanized.

In our program of research we have examined the power of humanization to counteract human aggression. Dehumanization can bring out the worst in people. I was struck in some experiments we conducted by how hard it is for people to behave inhumanely toward others if you personalize or humanize them a bit. The results of this research suggest that the power of humanization can be used to counteract inhumanities.

EVANS: Yes, that's true. But wouldn't some argue that a certain amount of dehumanization and depersonalization is a function of our society, by virtue of its very structure?

BANDURA: Yes. There are many aspects in our society that foster depersonalization. We have urbanization, mechanization, automation, a lot of mobility, so that people are relating to each other in much more impersonal ways. It is much easier to behave inhumanely toward someone who is non-personalized than toward someone whom you know.

fication involves an historical advantageous comparison, namely, you got your democracy through violence, why can't we get ours that way?

The third mechanism that works on the construal of the behavior operates through euphemistic language. People are skilled in using language to mask the reprehensible. In military situations, soldiers do not kill people, they "waste" them. We talk of "clean surgical bombing strikes" invoking the imagery of a curative metaphor. The women and children who are killed by bombs are "collateral damage." One cannot get too morally exercised over collateral damage.

Euphemisms are extensively used in everyday life when people have to do things that bring personal benefits but harm others. In such situations they preserve their self-esteem by characterizing what they do in benign language. Thus teaching business students how to lie in competitive transactions, the instructor calls it "strategic misrepresentation." The acid rain that is killing our lakes and forests loses its acidity when it is euphemistically called "atmospheric deposition of anthropogenically derived substances." It's pretty hard to get exercised over anthropogenically derived substances. Acid rain is a different story. Many people lost a good hunk of their retirement income in the recent economic meltdown in the stock market crash. The executive offices of a leading brokerage firm issued a memo labeling it as a "fourth-quarter equity retreat." Those whose cash flow was diminished have a quite different name for it.

Through euphemisms people couch culpable behavior in very acceptable terms. There's much use of passive agentless forms in verbiage, creating the appearance that culpable behavior is the work of nameless forces. There is no agent behind it. I got some amusing examples from police blotters of how people have described some of the accidents they got into. In this one case, the person, who wiped out a telephone pole, went on to say that he was driving his car and the telephone pole kept approaching and finally hit his front end. The telephone pole became the culpable agency. The athletic metaphor was extensively used in the Watergate criminal activity. The criminal conspiracy became "game plans" and the conspirators were "team players," who were "deep-sixing" documents, and so on. A tremendous amount of illegality and culpable behavior was being peddled under euphemistic labels.

These three mechanisms that operate on redefining behavior are the most powerful ones for moral disengagement because they not only disengage morality from culpable conduct, but engage self-approval for doing it well. To the extent that people are fully convinced that the enterprise is serving moral purposes, they take pride in being able to do it well.

Another set of moral disengagement mechanisms operates by distorting or obscuring the relation between actions and the harm they cause. Moral restraints are activated most strongly when there is a clear relation between action and detrimental consequences. So the way to disengage morality is to fuzzy up or obscure the sense of personal agency. This is achieved through displacement of responsibility. As long as an authority orders people to behave in a certain way, they do not feel personally resonsible for what they do. They are carrying out somebody else's orders and therefore they are not the initiators of the activity.

EVANS: It was kind of interesting that in my dialogue with Arthur Miller, the playwright, he came to grips with this very interesting situation of trying to look at this whole line of authority as an excuse for our acts which may, in fact, be immoral. He felt the lines of authority which were necessary to carry out the holocaust illustrates exactly what you're talking about. In fact, this is the theme of one of his plays.

BANDURA: Large-scale inhumanities are perpetrated through hierarchial social systems. The moral control of intermediaries is most easily disengaged because they do not formulate the policies, nor do they carry out the dirty work. They are removed from the injurious consequences of the actions and they

do not bear responsibility for the policy decisions. In logical experiments the authorization is explicit. But i no one in a position of power would be that stupid to transgressive behavior directly.

EVANS: No individual appears to be specifically responsibility for an order so no one can be blamed out the order.

BANDURA: Yes. In real life, authorities do n culpable behavior in a direct way that makes ther accountable. They avoid personal responsibility sons: First, if things go wrong no one wants to be resonsible for them, and second, authorizers wa their self-esteem. They do not want the blood inhumanities on their hands. So the displaceme bility tends to be done insidiously. Authorities nisms whereby the known remains unknown able remains unknowable. Activities are sanction leave considerable ambiguity about who autho activity is couched in euphemisms so that tho the policies are persuaded that it is serving a pose. The whole authorization process works than in Milgram's (1974) studies of obedience the experimenter commands subjects repeat nitively in the face of growing objections.

The second mechanism for obscuring p culpability is diffusion of resonsibilities. T sion making and division of labor, activit So people do not see their contribution as with the larger enterprise. Their attention their subpart well, rather than worrying a cations of the larger enterprise.

EVANS: But what about the victims of

BANDURA: Another set of disengage on how people view the victims of cu are two mechanisms at this level that

In psychological textbooks and in the media, the reports of Milgram's research on obedient aggression highlight how easy it is to get good people to do evil deeds. But what does not get mentioned is the power of humanization to counteract aggression. In Milgram's experiments when the participants were personalized a bit, or they had to express aggression directly rather than remotely, it was very difficult to persuade many of them to carry out the punitive acts. The experimenters had to browbeat them and many still refused to behave inhumanely. When the commands were issued by telephone, no one paid much attention to the orders. We tend to emphasize the more sensational negative findings, but rarely mention the power of personalization to counteract aggression experiments. Granted that we need to understand inhumanities because they can do us in, but it seems to me that the lesson on humanization is equally powerful and socially important.

Another self-exonerating factor at the level of the victim is the attribution of blame to the victim. In this process aggressors view themselves as an innocent party whose behavior is provoked by the victims, or compelled by external circumstances. By blaming the victims or circumstances, not only are one's actions excusable, but one can feel self-righteous in the mistreatment.

EVANS: Exactly the way rape victims are often treated, aren't they?

BANDURA: Yes. In fact, I analyzed how all these moral disengagement mechanisms operate in rape. At the level of social justification, rape occurs with high incidence in societies where the pattern of male dominance prevails, aggressive sexuality is valued as a sign of manliness, and women are treated as property. Rape is infrequent in more equalitarian societies. Macho ideologies and an ethic of male dominance foster rape and other forms of sexual abuse of women. Then there is attribution of blame to the victim, namely, women are held responsible for rapes because of their sexually exciting behavior or dress. Responsibility for rape is often displaced to biological drives. Men are not responsible for forced intercourse because their sexual drive made them do it. If you examine the rape myths, they tend to incorporate these different disengagement mechanisms, namely the attribution of blame to the victim, and the ideology of male dominance; they pervert the consequences of the rape. Rapists and those who subscribe to the rape myth believe that women secretly enjoy being sexually assaulted. Rapists twist a trauma into an unconscious sexual gratification. This mechanism operates on how the consequences of sexual assaults are viewed.

People are skilled in not finding adverse consequences of culpable behavior. And as long as they do not know the consequences of their injurious behavior, there is no reason for their morality to even be activated. Through misrepresentation or minimization of consequences events are construed in ways that moral sanctions are never activated.

EVANS: Using your earlier example of rape, then, the male rapist minimizes his crime by convincing himself that in fact the female victim was actually the instigator, perhaps even secretly enjoying the act itself.

BANDURA: Yes, that's exactly it. Rapists and those with a proclivity to rape believe that women secretly enjoy being raped.

So far I have described the model of moral disengagement at the personal level. But the disengagement mechanisms are usually orchestrated at the social level as well. To mobilize a populace for military action, leaders have to convince people of the morality of the national cause. The problem experienced by the veterans of the Vietnam War were aggravated because the nation was divided on the morality of that military involvement. Many people disputed the morality of that war. Those who had to fight it suffered personal and social consequences that were probably more severe than in any other war. They did not come back as heroes. They came back with the feeling that they were fighting a war that did not have moral justification.

To promote a humane society, one needs not only to instill humane codes in people, but to ensure that social systems support a humane society and do not misuse disengagement practices to enlist people for inhumane purposes. At the social level, we need to create control mechanisms so that social systems support compassionate behavior rather than inhumane activities. This is easier to achieve in a pluralistic system. A monolithic system can easily control the major sources of information and use them to justify and sanction large-scale inhumanities. In a system with political diversity, people question, argue, debate, and have a healthy skepticism of suspect moral appeals.

The issue of morality looms large in the area of nuclear deterrents. Most everyone agrees that a first strike is immoral, but there is considerable controversy about the morality of nuclear deterrents and nuclear weaponry. Proponents argue that a deterrent system is needed to protect the populace and that a society is morally obligated to protect its citizens from a nuclear attack. They distrust efforts at arms reduction on the grounds that their protagonists will cheat and verification procedures are inadequate.

Opponents of nuclear deterrents consider the development of nuclear bombs and even threats to use them as morally wrong. This is because unlike conventional weapons, nuclear weapons produce vast human and ecological devastation indiscriminately. A retaliatory strike would achieve only massive mutual annihilation. The devastating human and ecological toll would spread both within and across nations. The "just" war tenets are much more difficult to apply to nuclear weaponry because of their massive indiscriminate consequences. There is a self-destruct element to nuclear retaliation, namely, one destroys oneself as well as the enemy. Whoever is left in the aftermath would find themselves in a largely uninhabitable environment. A nuclear deterrence doctrine, paradoxically, seeks to achieve a deterrent effect with threats that none in their right mind could conceive of even using. So nations are involved in bluff games. They posture menacingly with nuclear weapons and growing escalation of ever-deadlier arsenals. No technical system is ever foolproof. As long as nuclear weapons exist there is always a risk that they may be fired accidentally or launched intentionally by enraged, panic-stricken, or suicidal leadership. On four occasions, the United States went into a state of nuclear war alert and only last-minute efforts revealed errors in the computer warning system. The issue of moral disengagement applies equally to what nations are going to do with the deadly arsenals they have created. Control of behavior by mutual threat is deeply entrenched in political and military doctrines. Human survival requires de-escalative modes of thinking and behaving. Clearly, the major challenge in the area of morality is the morality of nuclear weapons and deterrence doctrines.

EVANS: You may recall that Freud (1937) wrote a paper called, "Psychoanalysis Determinable, Indeterminable." What he said in that paper was something like: "As therapists I think we've done a pretty good job of learning how to make people dependent on us, but we still haven't been very effective in developing independence." And this has essentially been the problem in the area of behavior modification or almost any situation where ultimately we're hoping that some level of self-management is attained. You're looking at this issue as you develop your construct, self-efficacy, are you not?

BANDURA: Yes. Effective functioning requires that people develop competencies and skills. In addition, they need a strong self-belief in their own efficacy to put those skills to good use. Our views of ability and competence have changed in recent years. We used to conceptualize ability as a more or less fixed attribute that we possessed. It is evident from the efficacy research that people with the same skills can perform poorly, adequately or extraordinarily, depending on how well they orchestrate the subskills they have developed. Skills are a generative rather than a fixed capability and perceived efficacy plays a critical role in whether they are used well, poorly, or extraordinarily. I have been interested in the ways in which people's self-beliefs in their capabilities enable them to exercise some control over events that affect their lives and how self-belief translates into human accomplishments, motivation, and personal well-being. We have identified several different ways in which self-beliefs of efficacy affect psychological functioning. People's beliefs in their capabilities have a powerful effect on their choice behavior. They choose to engage in activities that they believe they can master and they tend to avoid activities and situations they believe exceed their coping capabilities.

EVANS: What are the principal aspects of self-efficacy which influence our lives?

BANDURA: Anything that affects choice behavior can have a profound effect on our life paths. Choices determine which

potentialities are cultivated and which remain undeveloped. Self-beliefs of efficacy also have a powerful effect on motivation. A high sense of efficacy leads people to mobilize a high level of effort in which they undertake and persevere in the face of obstacles and difficulties.

The third effect is concerned with how perceived self-efficacy affects thinking processes. When people encounter problems and obstacles, their thinking processes can be self-aiding or self-hindering. People who have a high sense of efficacy tend to devote their attention and cognitive resources to mastering the problems at hand, whereas people who are plagued by self-doubts about their efficacy tend to worry about all the things that can go wrong. If they are running off failure scenarios, they undermine their efforts. If they visualize success scenarios and effective courses of action they create positive guides for performance.

EVANS: How else does self-efficacy affect our psychological welfare and functioning?

BANDURA: The way in which efficacy affects psychological well-being and functioning is by altering vulnerability to stress and depression. People who have a low sense of coping efficacy are vulnerable to stress and depression when they encounter failures. The effects of perceived efficacy on emotional reactions involve not only perceptions of personal coping capabilities, but also perceptions that one can exercise control over one's own consciousness. It is not perturbing thoughts per se, but the perceived inefficacy to turn them off that accounts for high distress. This process of cognitive thought control is nicely captured in a proverb that says, "You can't prevent the birds of worry and care from flying over your head, but you can stop them from building a nest in your head." Thought control efficacy is also a key to the control of obsessional ruminations. The way in which self-efficacy contributes to the regulation of one's own consciousness is a fascinating issue.

4

Self-Efficacy

In this section, Dr. Bandura and I discuss his views of the role of competencies and skills in the individual and how they relate to the individual's level of self-efficacy. We discuss his conception of the major characteristics of perceived self-efficacy. We also discuss how he believes self-efficacy provides the resiliency for creative individuals to persist in gaining an objective even after being rejected many times. We also discuss his conception of the role of self-efficacy in the educational setting. Finally, Dr. Bandura and I discuss the recent work in psychoneuroimmunology and the role of perceived self-efficacy in health maintenance.

EVANS: In other words, the level of each individual's particular self-efficacy to a large degree dictates how well he/she will function as a person, how he/she will handle stresses, how well he/she copes and even, to a degree, his/her level of motivation. It's a rather progressive situation, with several factors coming into play to move the individual towards his own personal state of well-being, isn't it?

BANDURA: Yes, the processes are enlisted in getting from self-belief to behavior, motivation, and psychological well-being. A robust sense of self-efficacy is required for personal well-being and achievement. The reason for this is that our normative social realities are full of obstacles, frustrations, failures, impediments, setbacks, and inequities. The common reality is really pretty lousy. People must have a robust sense of their efficacy to sustain the perseverant effort needed to succeed. If people abort their efforts prematurely, you are not going to achieve much. Most successes do not come easily. They come through perseverant effort and many failed attempts. A resilient sense of personal efficacy provides the necessary staying power. There is a delightful book by John White (1982) called *Rejection*, in which he graphically demonstrates that the striking characteristics of people who have achieved eminence in different fields include an inextinguishable sense of self-efficacy combined with a strong belief in the worth of what they are doing. He documents how many of the literary classics brought their authors repeated rejection, especially early in their careers. Rejection is the rule rather than the exception. The novelist Saroyan accumulated about 3,000 rejections before he had his first piece published. Gertrude Stein was submitting poems for twenty years before she had her first one accepted. Now that's invincible self-efficacy. James Joyce's *The Dubliners* (1954) was rejected by twenty-two publishing houses. E. E. Cummings had one of his book manuscripts repeatedly rejected. When he finally got it published, the dedication read, "With no thanks to . . . "—and he listed the dozen publishing houses written in uppercase. I might add it was his mother who finally published the book.

EVANS: A good sense of humor doesn't hurt either, does it?

BANDURA: Not at all. A sense of humor also helps endurance. One resilient author wallpapered his apartment with rejection slips. He preferred the "8 x 11" ones to the "3 x 5" ones, because he could cover a larger area. He threw rejection parties in which he sent invitations on the back of his surplus rejection slips.

Early rejection is also the rule rather than the exception in other creative endeavors. The Impressionists could not get any of their paintings exhibited in the Paris salons. They finally set up their own competitive shows. Early in Picasso's career, an art dealer would not allow him to bring his pictures in from out of the rain. Van Gogh sold only one painting during his lifetime. The portrait of Whistler's mother was condemned by the Royal Art Academy for nineteen years to a cellar for rejected artwork. She was finally resurrected and sold to a pawnbroker for a few pounds. Now she hangs majestically in the Louvre.

Renowned composers have not fared any better. Stravinsky was run out of town when he first served the Parisians *The Rite of Spring*. Frank Lloyd Wright was one of the more severely rejected and criticized architects through much of his career. To turn to more familiar examples, Hollywood rejected Fred Astaire as "a skinny, balding person who could dance a bit." Decca Records rejected The Beatles with the rejective pronouncement: "We don't like their sound, and guitars are on the way out." Whoever issued that non-prophetic evaluation probably cringes at each sight of a guitar. The rejection list goes on.

EVANS: Of course, but rejection isn't unique to just the arts. Even in our own field we can see it, can't we?

BANDURA: It is not unusual for scientific classics to suffer repeated rejection. The striking example in psychology is John

Garcia (Garcia, J., & Koelling, R. A., 1966). His contributions are now well-recognized, but early in his career his manuscripts were consistently rejected because his findings did not conform to the common belief concerning conditioning processes. It is bad enough to get your manuscripts rejected, but when the rejections come with hostile embellishments, it is more difficult to take. Garcia was once told by one of the reviewers of his manuscript that one is no more likely to find the phenomenon that Garcia discovered than bird droppings in a cuckoo clock. With those kinds of verbal droppings one has to have a very robust sense of efficacy to continue the pursuit for new muses.

The same thing happens with physical technologies that are ahead of their time. The period between the introduction of a beneficial physical technology and its widespread adoption is a long time. The moral of the Book of Rejections is that people should not be too quick to attribute rejection to personal failings. To do so might be self-limiting.

EVANS: But success, particularly early success, isn't a guarantee for personal happiness. Just look at the incidence of post-award depression in Nobel Prize laureates.

BANDURA: That is an interesting issue in creativity. What happens to people who experience spectacular success early in their careers? They cannot help but use that remarkable accomplishment for self-comparison of future attainments. We often emphasize the negative effects of unfavorable social comparison. But there is also a problem with self-comparison when you have a spectacular early achievement. Later creativity may not match the early success.

Linus Pauling was once asked, "What do you do after you win a Nobel Prize?" He said, "You change fields, of course!" A change of pursuits breaks the unfavorable self-comparison. It is not all that uncommon for Nobel laureates to go through a period of depression if they judge that their subsequent work never measured up to the quality of the early achievement that won them the Nobel Prize. Irving Berlin put it well when he said, "The toughest thing about success is you have to continue to be successful." His observation captured the pressure that success may create and the way in which self-comparison to early spectacular successes can instill doubts about one's own capabilities.

EVANS: In your work on self-efficacy, Dr. Bandura, could you relate some of this work to an obvious application—the field of education? I'm wondering if you'd like to talk a little bit about that because it seems like such a relevant area to the subject of self-efficacy.

BANDURA: There are three levels at which self-efficacy theory has been applied to cognitive development. The first application is concerned with how children's perceived efficacy affects their rate of learning. Dale Schunk and I (Bandura & Schunk, 1981) collaborated on one project in which we addressed the motivational and self-efficacy problems of children who presented severe deficits in mathematical skills. We devised a program grounded in efficacy theory to test whether we could develop mathematical competencies, build children's sense of learning efficacy, and alter their level of interest in the subject matter. The program drew on the motivating power of proximal goal setting.

We selected youngsters who had virtually no confidence in their arithmetic ability. We developed a program of self-directed instruction that explained the necessary mathematical operations. One group of students pursued the self-directed study with daily subgoals of learning a different mathematical skill each day. A second group set a long-term goal of learning all the mathematical skills by a future date. Other students studied the course without any goals. We reasoned that attainable subgoals would raise and maintain motivation, and mastery of subgoals would build an increasing sense of mathematical efficacy. In contrast, distant goals make it difficult to gain a sense of mastery. Small progress pales by comparison to a distant standard of full mastery.

We found that under conditions of attainable subgoals children made faster progress, they gained greater confidence in their mathematical efficacy and they developed greater interest in mathematics than did students who tried to motivate themselves with only distant goals.

Schunk (1987; 1984) has conducted a large number of studies in which he superimposes on the self-directed instruction different social factors that could affect children's beliefs in their efficacy. Path analyses of causal linkages reveal that mastery of subject matter enhances children's beliefs in their efficacy, and perceived efficacy, in turn, increases persistence and academic achievement. Perceived efficacy contributes to achievement beyond the effects of ability. In these students efficacy theory was tested on a tough crowd, namely, children who not only were markedly deficient in skills but were disinterested in, and hated, the subject matter. A second level of application of self-efficacy theory to cognitive development examines how teachers' perceptions of their instructional efficacy affect children's academic progress.

EVANS: Incidentally, this would be a good opportunity to ask you to contrast the type of investigation which you undertook with Dale Schunk, and the kind of work that Robert Rosenthal (Rosenthal & Rubin, 1978, 1980; Rosenthal Jacobsen, 1968) generated—you know, with the so-called self-fulfilling prophecy "Pygmalion in the Classroom" study where teachers were provided with bogus reports of their students' potential performance. These studies seem to suggest that reports of high potential performance could lead to not only higher expectations of success, but higher degrees of success, as well. If I can understand what you've done with Dale Schunk, your finding is that if you believe you're good, you're more likely to show that you're good, just as Rosenthal seemed to observe, but there's something a little different introduced with your path analysis; you're really introducing another component to this process.

BANDURA: Yes, our research differs in the manner in which we develop children's academic competencies and perceived self-efficacy. There are four different ways of building self-efficacy. One is through mastery experiences. The second is through modeling. The third is through social persuasion—telling people that we have the capabilities to succeed. The fourth is based on judgments of physiological indicants of personal capabilities and vulnerabilities. These different sources of efficacy influences vary in their power to produce changes.

To build the children's sense of efficacy and academic competence we used the most powerful way of instilling self-efficacy—that is through personal mastery experiences. We equip the children with the cognitive skills and self-beliefs that enable them to succeed. The importance of self-belief is illustrated in the research by Janet Collins (1982). She selected children at three levels of mathematical ability—low, medium and high. Within each ability level, she picked children who had either a high or low sense of mathematical efficacy. She then gave them tough problems to solve. Ability level contributed to performance, but children's self-efficacy contributed independently to academic performance as well. Within each ability level, children who had a higher sense of efficacy solved more problems, they were more willing to go back and rework problems they had failed and were quicker to discard ineffective strategies. Intrinsic interest in mathematics was predicted by perceived self-efficacy but not by actual ability. Thus children who do poorly may do so because they lack the ability, or they have the ability but they lack the self-assurance to make good use of their skills. Self-doubts undermine the use of their skills.

So in our approach, we sought to promote two types of changes. We taught children the cognitive tools with which to achieve and, at the same time, we enhanced their sense of efficacy so that they can use those skills in effective ways.

EVANS: So going back to Rosenthal's "Pygmalion in the Classroom" study it more-or-less doesn't explore the process in sufficient depth?

BANDURA: They altered the teachers' perceptions of the children in the hope that it would start a positive process of change. Positive expectations would make the children more responsive to instruction which would produce a mutually reinforcing pattern to change.

A problem arises if you instill positive expectations in the teachers, but the children continue to perform poorly because they lack the basic skills and a low sense of competence to succeed. Disappointing progress can rapidly wipe out teachers' expectations. It is a question of how much power social persuasion alone can exert on this positive change process. Social persuasion alone is likely to produce variable results. If changing teachers' expectations produces quick results, the positive change will be initiated. If induction of positive expectations fails to produce quick successes, teachers will come to expect less of the children. So sometimes the expectancy manipulation works and sometimes it fails. It is difficult to build self-efficacy and competencies through social persuasion alone. One gains greater power over the process of change if, in addition to convincing children they have the capabilities to perform well, one can also structure challenges for them in such a way that they will experience a high level of success. You avoid placing them prematurely into situations where they're going to experience needless failure. This is especially important in early phases of skill development when people distrust their efficacy.

EVANS: By the way, some of these management seminars involving so-called success training seem to be missing that. I mean, it's as if this one element of actually having a success experience is not brought in I guess you'd say.

BANDURA: That's right. Perhaps I might illustrate this point with an example in sports. Bill Walsh, coach of the San Francisco football team, has been highly successful in developing quarterbacks. He is very skilled in building quarterbacks' sense of efficacy by inserting them gradually into situations where they are very likely to succeed. In this way, he not only builds the quarterback's self-confidence but also builds the teammates' confidence that the quarterback can produce good results. Words are cheap but it takes real skill in backing up social appraisals of capability with carefully structured performance tasks that are likely to bring success.

There is no shortage of entrepreneurs busily selling inner bliss, mind power, longevity, and visions of elegant life styles. They are exploiting what someone once called the law of molasses. If there is demand, there shall be supply. The different modes of building efficacy involve a process of providing people with genuine mastery experiences. These experiences must be structured in such a way that they will be maximally persuasive. They provide efficacy-demonstrating tests. One does not accomplish this readily by words alone.

I should also mention that there is a difference between saying and believing. Simply repeating that one has a capability is not necessarily self-convincing, especially when it contradicts existing strong beliefs. No amount of saying that I can fly will persuade me that I can get myself airborne. Self-beliefs of efficacy are affected by the authenticity of the efficacy information on which they are based. Self-beliefs built through mastery experiences are likely to remain strong and resistant to adversity. Weak self-beliefs are highly vulnerable to change. Self-doubts quickly mount in the face of difficulties and failures quickly reinstate distrust in one's capabilities.

EVANS: So, now, for example, in our own research (Evans, 1976; Evans, R. I. Rozell, R. M., Mittelmark, M. B., Hansen, W. B., Bane, A. L., & Havis, J., 1978; Evans, R. I., Rozelle, R. M., Maxwell, S. E., Raines, B. E., Dill, C. A., Guthrie, T. J., Henderson, A. H., & Hill, P. C., 1981) where we applied some of your social learning concepts as we developed the "Just Say No" social innoculation coping strategy in preventing the use of cigarettes; obviously, if we had just stopped at teaching "Just Say No," the way the current media slogans are misrepresenting our research, it wouldn't be enough. We provided for the adolescents in our studies at least simulated experiences where the teenagers actually acted out situations of "Just Saying No" and the other refusal coping strategies which we developed.

BANDURA: Yes. This point is well illustrated in powerful programs based on social learning principles that are being applied in organizational settings. People often get promoted to managerial or supervisory positions on the basis of their technical competence. But once they get promoted to that level, their success depends on their ability to work through people and inspire and motivate them. They often get promoted for technical reasons but their success resides in interpersonal skills.

Mastery modeling programs have been devised to instill supervisory competencies. The programs that are powerful have three basic components. Videotape modeling is used to present prototypic problem situations. Effective ways of dealing with them are modeled in easily mastered steps. Modeling transmits knowledge about the skills and strategies needed to work effectively with people. The modeling aids are designed to build self-assurance as well as to convey skills.

After participants understand the new skills, they need opportunities to perfect them. This is best done under simulated conditions where they need not worry about making mistakes or looking silly. In this second phase they gain proficiency in translating their knowledge into effective skills. This is usually achieved by role-playing difficult situations. They enact these situations and receive informative feedback as to where they are succeeding and where they are having problems.

The third phase involves a transfer program in which the trainees deal with the problems they encounter in their work. They are given a series of performance tasks each week to carry out on the job. They try their hand at them and come back and discuss where they succeeded and where they failed. If they still have problems, the subskills are modeled for them and they perfect them. So powerful programs transmit the required competencies, provide a setting in which to perfect the skills and then program the success experiences needed to apply the skills to the everyday environment. When you combine those three components you have a reliably effective change program.

EVANS: Now, going back for a moment to self-efficacy in the context of formal education, you alluded to modifying efficacy levels in teachers and how this affected their students.

BANDURA: Gibson and Dembo (1984) conducted an interesting study in which they measured teachers' perceived instructional efficacy on two dimensions. The first assessed teachers' beliefs that they were able to motivate and promote learning in difficult students. The second dimension assessed the extent to which the teachers believed that their educational effort will have some impact on children's educational development. Some teachers believe that no matter what you do in the school, adverse community or home conditions will wipe out any educational gains. Other teachers believe that one can have a significant impact on children's educational development regardless of what the environmental conditions might be.

Gibson and Dembo selected teachers who had a high sense of efficacy. They believed that children, however difficult they may be, are reachable and teachable, and that instructional efforts would produce lasting benefits. The low efficacy teachers expressed a low sense of capability that they could motivate and instruct difficult children, and even it they did, whatever changes they produced would not survive for long.

They then observed how these teachers actually operated in their classrooms. They found rather striking differences in the kinds of educational atmospheres that they were creating in their classrooms. The teacher with a high sense of efficacy spent more time on academic subject matters, whereas the low efficacy teachers devoted more time to nonacademic pastimes. High efficacy teachers stuck with children when they had difficulties, helped them succeed and then praised them for coming through. When low efficacy teachers called on children who did not come up with answers, they quickly gave up on them and criticized them.

Ashton and Webb (1986) measured the long-term effects of teachers' perceived instructional efficacy on children's academic achievement. They correlated the teachers' level of perceived efficacy with the degree of educational gain the children achieved over the course of the year, with control for entering ability level. The higher the teachers' sense of instructional efficacy, the higher was the children's level of educational gain as measured by standardized tests in mathematics, language and reading. This evidence shows that the perceived instructional efficacy of teachers has a cumulative effect.

The third level of analysis is concerned with the perceived efficacy of the school as a whole. The school is the unit of analyses rather than the individual teacher. This gets at the issue of how collective efficacy of schools fosters academic achievements of students in those schools.

Louise Parker and I have been developing a methodology for measuring collective efficacy and relating it to a social cognitive theory of organizational functioning. Organizations vary in the degree of interdependent effort needed to produce organizational results. In some group activities the members coordinate their efforts but work separately, in other activities the members have to work closely together to produce results.

EVANS: In other words, this could move into collective efficacy in organizational behavior which has been of interest to industrial-organizational psychologists among others.

BANDURA: There are three aspects of social cognitive theory that have relevance to organizational behavior. One is the use of mastery modeling to develop managerial competencies. The second is the use of goal systems to guide and motivate group effort. The third is concerned with the role of perceived efficacy in the level of functioning of an organization, especially the perceived efficacy of decision makers. However, the perceived efficacy of the organization as a whole has received little study.

The staffs of successful schools, whether they serve advantaged or disadvantaged students, have a strong sense of their efficacy to promote learning and high resiliency of perceived efficacy in the face of difficult realities. The teachers have a strong belief that the children are reachable and teachable and they achieve good results.

In this initial effort we are testing two approaches to collective efficacy. The first combines each teacher's personal efficacy to promote learning in the children. The second combines the teachers' beliefs about the capabilities of the school as a whole to achieve educational gains.

EVANS: Let's consider an example of collective efficacy of an outstanding university research group, led by a scientist who has just been awarded the Nobel Prize. You have here working together for a number of years a collection of research fellows, research associates, and so on. Someone new joins the group. The collective efficacy at the time of entry of this new person may have been developed in part because of this recognition for its leader in winning the Nobel Prize. This new researcher joining this group, one way or the other, is going to be influenced. How do you see the collective efficacy of an already existing group affecting a new member joining that group?

BANDURA: If you have a strong group sense of efficacy, the members will tackle intractable problems and have a good chance of finding solutions to them. That should boost the belief of a new member that tough problems are solvable. Group successes should have beneficial effects on the perceived efficacy of members. I was especially interested in studying schools because there are multiple schools, they all perform the same functions, and they provide standardized performance measures, namely, the level of educational gain the children achieved in language, reading, and mathematics.

EVANS: You're constantly monitoring gain.

BANDURA: That's right. We also measure the extent to which the efficacy of the principal sets the tone for the efficacy of the school. What happens to teachers' efficacy as they enter systems with high or low collective efficacy? We are finding that the longer the teachers teach in a high-efficacy school, the higher their sense of personal efficacy, whereas the longer teachers teach in a low-efficacy school, the lower their sense of instructional efficacy. These results seem to reflect group processes of mutual demoralization and mutual enhancement. A lot of social interaction, such as team planning and teaching, in a high-efficacy school's team is positively related to perceived collective efficacy. A lot of team teaching and planning in low-efficacy schools diminishes perceived collective efficacy. Fascinating group processes become researchable once a good methodology is developed. Important advances in a field often rest on significant methodological developments.

EVANS: Your recent election to the Institute of Medicine of the National Academy of Sciences is a significant recognition of your contributions to the bio-medical sciences. So let's move into another area of application relating to this recognition. This area, which is one of the fundamental challenges to the broader field of behavioral medicine, is psychoneuroimmunology. As you probably know there was an article not too long ago in the *New England Journal of Medicine* (1985) that took to task much of this work, particularly research in the cancer area such as that of the Simontons. The Simontons' work involves the use of cognitive imagery with patients who are trained to literally visualize their body fighting off cancerous cells. In the case of terminal cancer, criteria for success here might be merely prolongation of life rather than recovery. The Simontons would report an occasional remission at one extreme, or no effect of this technique at the other end except in terms of quality of life of the patient. With respect to quality of life, reports of patients in the group setting which the Simontons provide, suggest, in fact, that quality of life is improved, that patients feel more uplifted, less depressed. Rather than feelings of hopelessness, they report feelings of hope. I was called by *Smithsonian Magazine* some time ago to write a critique of this work and I decided not to do it because I wasn't really quite sure what critique I could provide in terms of a conceptually precise psychoneuroimmunologic model. What do you think about this work and the attack on it and the whole field of psychoneuroimmunology by the *New England Journal of Medicine* (1985) article?

BANDURA: I am very dubious that people can directly image themselves into health. Imaged metaphoric combat between immune killer cells and invading cancer cells severely strains credibility.

EVANS: Now, of course, more precise work in this area is being undertaken by individuals such as Janet Kiecolt-Glaser. (Kiecolt-Glaser, J. K., Glaser, R., Williger, D., Stout, J., Messick, G., Sheppard, S., Ricker, D., Romisher, S. C., Birner, W., Bonnell, G., & Donnerberg, R., 1985; Kiecolt-Glaser, J. K., Glaser, R., Strain, E. C., Stout, J. C., Tarr, K. L., Holliday, J. E., & Speicher, C. E., 1986; Kiecolt-Glaser, J. K., Glaser, R., 1987)

BANDURA: I'm familiar with this work. This is a fruitful line of research demonstrating that academic and interpersonal stressors can impair the immune system.

EVANS: Before you answer my question, let me briefly review this work in a somewhat more rigorous framework for the reader. In the Simontons' (Simonton, S., Matthews, O. C., & Simonton, S., 1982) type of clinical study there is no *direct* measure of the effects of the treatment on the immune system. In the case of Janet Kiecolt-Glaser, she's working with her husband who's an immunologist. They measured antibodies in the blood under double blind control conditions. They did not know the social manipulation under which the subject's blood is being tested. They've found exposure to stressful life events such as divorce on married couples and final examination week on students, resulted in measurable evidence of deteriorating function of the immune system. She also points out that another operant variable might be social support. For example, the immune systems of married versus single individuals appear to reflect the positive effects of social support.

Other studies along the same lines are reflected in the work of Redford Williams (1987) at Duke with patients who were about to undergo angiography. There was again a double blind condition. Angiographic findings suggested that the male patients who seemed to be lacking in social support were more likely to have significant coronary artery blockage than those who did not lack such support.

We obviously do not understand the mechanism operating here, or whether it is operating at the neurological, physiological or psychological level. How can self-efficacy be brought in as a variable in this type of research if, in fact, it is a factor?

BANDURA: There is a growing body of evidence that controllability is a key organizing principle regarding the nature of stress effects. In studies with animals, Maier and his colleagues (Maier, Landenslager, and Ryan, 1985) subjected animals to physical stressors under conditions where they could turn them off or they received the same physical stressors for the same duration except they could not exercise any control over them. Animals subjected to uncontrollable stressors showed impairment to the immune system's function.

EVANS: So this line of research which attempts to relate control to the function would seem to be a more attractive alternative means of exploring self-efficacy in the context of such research.

BANDURA: Yes, it established psychobiologic linkages between uncontrollability, stress and immune function. At the human level, for ethical reasons researchers cannot go around impairing people's immune systems with arbitrary stressors. So we have relied on correlational or quasi-experimental studies. In the correlational studies, life stressors are related to the incidence of infectious illnesses and changes in immune function. In the quasi-experimental studies, immune function is measured before and during medical school examinations as you briefly described earlier. Kiecolt-Glaser finds that periods of high stress impair different components of cellular immune function.

In our laboratory, we have been studying how perceived

coping self-efficacy affects biochemical processes that regulate immune function. We have been able to establish clear psychobiological linkages between efficacy and basic biological systems with phobic stressors. The participants in the research have experienced high levels of stress for years as a result of their phobic dread. With our powerful guided mastery treatment we can eliminate phobias in all participants in a couple of hours. This enables us to study biochemical reactions when people are exposed to the same phobic stressors with a low sense of coping efficacy and after their perceived self-efficacy is raised to the maximal level. All the participants gain lasting relief from phobic stressors while contributing to basic knowledge.

In one such study, conducted with Jack Barchas, Barr Taylor and Lloyd Williams (1985), we measured the effects of perceived coping efficacy on the activation of catecholamines. They are neurotransmitters and stress-related hormones. Phobics attempted to perform coping tasks in their low, medium and high perceived self-efficacy range. When they coped with phobic stressors in this high efficacy range they showed no catecholamine elevation. But when they coped with phobic stressors involving tasks for which they doubted their coping efficacy, they exhibited substantial increases of epinephrine and norepinephrine. After their perceived coping efficacy was strengthened to the maximal level by guided mastery treatment, they performed the same coping tasks without any differential activation of catecholamines. In earlier studies we demonstrated that a low sense of efficacy in coping with psychological stressors is accompanied by subjective distress and autonomic arousal as measured by accelerated heart rate and elevated blood pressure.

Another study with Delia Cioffi and Barr Taylor (Bandura, A., Cioffi, D. M., Taylor, C. B., & Brouillard, M. E., 1988), examined the effects of perceived self-efficacy in coping with cognitive stressors on the endogenous opioid system. This biochemical effect is of a special interest because the capacity of stress to impair the immune system is mediated, at least in part, by endogenous opioids. We selected cognitive stressors for study because a great deal of human stress arises from the strains of work loads exceeding cognitive capabilities. Our findings confirmed that perceived inefficacy to exercise control over cognitive stressors activates endogenous opioid systems.

The degree to which uncontrollable stressors affect the immune system depends on their intensity of chronicity. Much human stress is generated in the course of developing and expanding personal competencies. Stress activated while acquiring coping efficacy may have very different effects than high stress experienced with no hope of any relief. It would not be evolutionarily advantageous if acute stressors always impaired immune function. If this were the case, people would be highly vulnerable to infections. There are substantial evolutionary benefits to experiencing enhanced immune function during development of coping capabilities vital for effective adaptation. To explore this interesting issue, Sue Wiedenfeld, Anne O'Leary and I (Wiedenfeld, S. A., O'Leary, A., Bandura, A., & Brown, S., submitted) measured the immune function of phobics during a baseline phase, while they were gaining coping mastery over their phobia, and after they had achieved maximal perceived efficacy. We found that rapid development of strongly perceived efficacy to control phobic stressors increased immune function. These are some illustrations of how we are gaining better understanding of the biochemical mediators of psychosocial influences on health.

There are three possible pathways by which you might get linkages between coping self-efficacy and immune function. One would be the pathway I have just described. Perceived coping inefficacy creates subjective stress, autonomic arousal, and catecholamine and opioid activation. These biochemical mediators are now linked to immune function. This is the stress mediation pathway.

The second is the depression mediated pathway. People who have a low sense of efficacy for cultivating and maintaining social relationships that provide support systems and buffers against stressors are more vulnerable to depression. People who judge themselves as incapable of achieving certain levels of performance which they regard as indices of self-worth, are also vulnerable to depression. There's evidence that people who are lonely or depressed show immune suppression. So there can be a linkage between perceived inefficacy, depression and impaired immune function.

The third possible path of influence is through expectancy learning. Ader (Ader, R., & Cohen, N., 1981) has shown that immune reactions are subject to expectancy learning. After environmental events are paired with substances that affect immune function, the environmental events alone begin to affect immune responses. This mode of influence operates through the central neural link. In some of our research we have shown that situationally activated self-expectations of coping efficacy produce anticipatory physiological reactions that can have some impact on immune function. So three pathways may be involved—through stress mediation, depression mediation, and central modulation by expectancy learning.

EVANS: We've discussed earlier the role of social support in affecting the immune system. I. G. Sarason (Sarason, I. G., Sarason, B. R., & Pierce, G. R., 1988) reviewed the various measures of social support. It's really surprising how many people are now measuring this in a different way.

The point that one might make is that the term "social support," at best, is a rather broad term measured in various ways. Could we have a spectrum of social support that is so low in quality it is almost aversive? Some of these more descriptive indicators of social support may not tell the whole story at all. Like in the Redford Williams (1987) study we mentioned earlier which reported that single men were more likely to have cardiovascular disease than the married men. But these are global, demographic data that he is analyzing. In terms of trying to analyze the relation between social support and something operating as subtly as the development of plaque in the blood vessels presents a real problem.

BANDURA: Social support would have beneficial effects if it provides a buffer against stressors. But like most influences, its effects will depend on its nature and quality. The presence of people who are sources of conflict is more likely to be stressful than tranquilizing. Some people may model and encourage the very detrimental behavior one wishes to change. Highly supportive drinking buddies will not be of much help to a person struggling with the stress of alcohol-related problems. The question is the direction in which social support operates. I might illustrate this with research I have conducted with Robert DeBusk and Barr Taylor on post-coronary rehabilitation. It turns out that about 60 percent of the people who have had coronaries have uncomplicated ones. Their heart heals and they are physically capable to resume an active life. But their recovery is slow because they believe they have an impaired heart. They now fear that if they exert themselves they will have another heart attack. As a result, they restrict their activities and social life, they may have difficulty getting back to work, and they fear that sexual activities will do them in.

There is not much one can do for them physically. The rehabilitative task is to convince people who have had a minor heart attack that their cardiovascular capacity is strong enough to resume an active, productive life. Cardiologists informally use the four modes of efficacy induction. They may use the treadmill exercise device to demonstrate to patients how much stamina they have; in terms of modeling, they may bring in ex-patients who demonstrate how they are leading active, productive lives. As for social persuasion, physicians use their expertise to persuade patients of their physical capabilities. In the physiological mode, they try to correct patients' tendencies to misread their physiology so they do not misattribute all their aches, pains, fatigues and windedness to an impaired heart when it could be that these sensations may reflect their inactivity.

We decided to test formally the impact of two of these modes of efficacy induction on recovery of cardiovascular capacity. The first used the treadmill to demonstrate to patients their cardiac capabilities. We devised specific efficacy measures of patients' beliefs about how much strain their heart could tolerate; how much physical activity and emotional strain they could handle; and their perceived capability to engage in sexual activity.

We put patients on the treadmill and had them master progressively heavier workloads. They were told that the strain put on their heart in the treadmill test far exceeded any strain that might be put on the heart by their everyday activities.

Recovery from a heart attack is a social, rather than an individual matter. This brings us to the issue of social support. All the patients were males. The wives' beliefs about their husbands' physical and cardiac capabilities may aid or retard the recovery process. We decided to test whether we could change the spouse's belief about her husband's cardiovascular capacity. They all believed that their husbands had a weak heart that could not tolerate any strain and stress. The wives participated in three different conditions in the study. They were present to observe their husband's stamina as he performed the treadmill; or the wives observed the treadmill test and then performed the treadmill exercises themselves to gain firsthand information of the physical stamina it requires. That was a compelling way of demonstrating that their husband has a tough heart. After these activities, couples were informed by the cardiologist about the patients' cardiac functioning and their capacity to resume activities in their daily lives. The patient's and spouse's perceptions of his physical and cardiac capabilities were measured before and after the treadmill activity, and again after the medical counseling.

When wives were not present or only observed the treadmill test they continued to believe that their husbands had a very vulnerable heart. The counseling by the cardiology staff did not change their beliefs. Wives who had personally experienced the cardiovascular strain imposed by the treadmill judged their husbands' treadmill accomplishments as reflecting a tough heart. These wives were also highly receptive to the cardiologist's reassurance that their husbands could lead an active life.

The direction the social support takes is partly determined

by perceived efficacy. If the wife believes that her husband has an impaired heart, her social support will take the form of protecting him from physical activity. Whereas, if the wife has a strong belief that her husband has a robust heart, her social support would take the form of encouraging him to become more active. Pursuit of an active life improves patients' cardiac capabilities. Indeed, when we conducted a six-month follow-up test, we found that the best predictor of recovery of cardiovascular capacity was the joint perceived efficacy of husband and wife that he had a robust heart system. These findings suggest that social support can work in the direction of fostering the recovery process or hindering it.

EVANS: I think that little touch of having the wife try it for herself is a most interesting component of this study.

BANDURA: It was an intervention that took 15 minutes and had a profound effect as reflected in follow-up measures of recovery of cardiovascular capacity.

EVANS: We've already been discussing the involvement of self-efficacy in some specific areas of health research. It would be interesting how you perceive the application of efficacy theory to the health field in general. What thoughts do you have about this?

BANDURA: Self-efficacy theory has been applied to the health field at two levels. The first level that I just described is concerned with the impact of perceived efficacy on biochemical mediators of health and illness. The second level is aimed at clarifying how perceived efficacy affects the adoption of protective health habits.

EVANS: Here we're talking about prevention.

BANDURA: Yes. Perceived self-efficacy aids adoption of health-promoting behaviors and control of risky health habits in three ways: First, it affects whether or not people even consider adopting healthy practices. Those who have a low sense of efficacy do not even try and if they try, they are quick to abandon their efforts if they do not achieve quick successes. Health communications are used extensively to persuade people to alter their risky habits. They often try to motivate people to change by arousing fear about the ravages of disease. Findings show that people's perceived efficacy that they could stick to the preventive behavior is a good predictor of whether they adopt the health-promoting habit. Fear arousal has little effect. The implication of this research is that health messages should place greater emphasis on conveying the belief that people have the capability to exercise some control over their habits rather than trying to scare them into health. The higher the induced perceived self-efficacy, the more likely are people to adopt the recommended practices.

The second efficacy effect is concerned with how much benefit people derive from treatments for physical disorders. The more the treatments raise people's perceived efficacy that they can exercise some control over their condition, the more they benefit from them. Perceived self-efficacy has been shown to enhance change across a wide variety of conditions, including postcoronary recovery, reduction of pain and dysfunction of arthritis, reduction of tension headaches, control of childbirth pain, stress reduction, weight and cholesterol reduction, control over bulemic behavior, adherence to exercise programs, management of safe sex practices to avoid sexually transmitted diseases, and control of addictive habits that impair health.

The third way in which perceived self-efficacy affects health is in the maintenance of changed health habits—it strengthens durability of changes and reduces vulnerability to relapse. The area that has been studied most extensively is the maintenance of smoking cessation. Even though smokers have quit smoking, not everyone feels a high enough sense of efficacy that they can resist smoking in certain pressure situations. Perceived self-efficacy at the end of treatment predicts which participants will relapse and how soon they will relapse. The efficacy research on maintenance processes highlights the need to equip people with self-regulatory skills and self-belief in their capability to motivate themselves and exercise control over their behavior. Each of the modes of efficacy influence can be used to develop the resilient sense of efficacy needed to override future difficulties. These include mastery over high-risk situations, modeling influences that demonstrate how to reinstate control should a setback occur and show that success requires tenacious efforts, and persuasory influences that lead people to view a slip as a temporary setback rather than an inherent personal deficiency.

EVANS: Now turning to the AIDS problem, how do you view it?

BANDURA: Most of the effort to gain some control over the spread of AIDS has centered on health communications. This is just the first component of an effective change program—getting factual information to people. Even this minimal effort has been weak because it is often couched in euphemisms. Our society has never been able to talk straight about sex. The health messages talk about exchange of "bodily fluids." Now, there are a lot of bodily fluids. Such euphemistic messages can instill public phobias for bodily fluids that are quite safe.

EVANS: Yes, you sort of wonder what a phrase like that really means to some of the people out there who are highly at risk for getting AIDS and may be in some lower educational levels.

BANDURA: By now most people know which behavioral practices carry high risk for AIDS infection. But some continue to engage in them because they have a belief system that performing some ritual will transform risky habits to safe ones. These misbeliefs include: showering before and after sexual contact reduces the risk, if partners have no lesions they are safe, or a small number of partners provides safety. Health communication messages must address misbeliefs that lead informed people to continue to engage in high-risk practices.

The second aspect of AIDS prevention recognizes that following safer sex practices is a problem of managing interpersonal and sexual relationships when the mode of transmission is sexual. People need to develop skills on how to negotiate safer sex practices. How do you broach the subject? What do you say and do if the partner resists the protective practices? How do you negotiate such conflicts? Interpersonal relationships often involve power differentials. Other factors, such as emotional and economic dependence, coercive threat, fear of rejection, and subcultural role prescriptions, make it difficult to insist on safer sex practices. People need modeling and simulated practice on how to exercise ill-protective control in social relationships. Risky drug injection practices similarly involve complicating social influences and personal skills for dealing with them. Just providing information will not instill competencies.

AIDS prevention requires a broad approach, aimed at altering social norms and subcultural patterns. Most intravenous drug users who use contaminated needles do not move in traditional social networks. Nontraditional social networks must be enlisted for high-risk groups that are beyond the reach of the usual community organizations. The AIDS epidemic, spread through the gay community, then crossed over via bisexuals and intravenous drug users to heterosexual transmission of the virus to their female sexual partners who, in turn, run a high risk of infecting their infants through perinatal transmission. AIDS is taking an increasing toll on women and children, especially among ethnic minorities in impoverished settings where drug use is prevalent. Community approaches are needed to curb this spread of AIDS.

EVANS: This leads us back to the discussion of your work on morality. Here again is a dilemma. By some standards of morality, sexual behavior itself is constrained. For example, an evangelist who argues that the answer to the AIDS problem is abstinence. What he is really suggesting is that there's an acceptable, moral way to stop this problem, and essentially that it is immoral to utilize more direct persuasion techniques to deal directly with practices and behaviors that would be involved in avoiding contagion. I was wondering if you'd like to comment on this since this kind of dilemma certainly could be a very destructive aspect of stemming the spread of AIDS.

BANDURA: They seem to be more concerned with curbing sex practices they find morally objectionable than in curbing the spread of the epidemic by increasing the safety of sex.

EVANS: But the way it's handled, though, creates a moral dilemma for the parents of these children and for public health officials who are supposedly the ones who have to encourage educators and school board members to include "safe sex" information in the school curriculum.

BANDURA: The problem in educating the public on how to safeguard against infection by the AIDS virus is that our major dissemination institutions do not want to touch the issue. Television resists getting into the act for fear that talk of protective sex practices will alienate some of their viewers and jeopardize advertising revenue. They don't want it. As you pointed out, it is difficult to conduct preventive programs in the schools. Efforts to provide sex education in the school has had a stormy history. Some factions of the society sought to maintain a veil of silence about protective sexual practices on the belief that such information will promote indiscriminate sexuality.

EVANS: —or even certain aspects of almost any kind of educational program that seem to obviously be in conflict with prevailing moral values in a community—

BANDURA: Before the AIDS epidemic, there was an active movement to bar psychological procedures from schools. Even role-playing which is an important element in peer modeling programs to teach resistance to peer pressure for injurious activities was on the hit list. The AIDS issue has become highly politicized. So I am not optimistic that the television industry or the school system will do much to inform the public and teach them how to safeguard against infection from the AIDS virus. Our society does not provide much in the way of treatment of drug addiction, nor is it about to mount preventive

programs for refractory drug users on safe drug injection practices. Lack of social consensus places the burden on local initia-
tives. For example, in an outreach program, Watters (1987) had
street counselors teach intravenous drug users how to reduce
the risk of AIDS by disinfecting needles with ordinary house-
hold bleach which kills the virus. The disinfection procedure,
which had rarely been used before, was widely adopted and
consistently applied. It is commonly believed that drug users
are too driven by their addiction to take the time to protect
themselves. The high adoption of self-protective practices contradicts this image. Indeed, some drug addicts from Oakland
came all the way to San Francisco to pick up the information
and a supply of bleach. The street counselors also helped them
with referrals to drug treatment programs. It is more difficult
to get people to relinquish behavior that is powerfully rein-
forced than to adopt safer forms of the behavior. For those drug
users who refuse treatment, society condemns many women
and children to this deadly disease if it refuses to give drug
users protective knowledge and the means with which to cur-
tail this spread of AIDS.

5

Reactions to Criticism, A Recent Book

In this section, Dr. Bandura and I discuss his reactions to some of the criticism of his work, particularly the rejection of causal cognition by the radical behaviorists. Finally, he briefly discusses his recent book, Social Foundations of Thought and Action.

EVANS: Dr. Bandura, as we close our discussion, it might be interesting to hear what criticisms of your work have troubled you the most.

BANDURA: Well, you cannot allow criticism to perturb you too much, because it will either drive you to the sauce or distort your scholarship. Conforming to what is in vogue will not ruffle any feathers, nor will it advance the field much.

I receive critical salvos from radical behaviorists who believe that thought has no causal influence on how we feel or behave. From their perspective, the inclusion of cognitive processes in the analysis of human behavior is a regressive step. It is amusing to see radical behaviorists, who contend that thoughts have no causal influence, devoting considerable time to speeches, articles, and books in an effort to convert people's beliefs to their way of thinking. This vigorous advocacy is self-contradictory but understandable because what people believe affects what they do. Radical behaviorists rely on several arguments for dismissing the causal role of cognition.

One line of reasoning strips thought of any causal influence by rechristening it. Thoughts and beliefs are simply renamed verbal behavior. It is then argued that behavior does not cause behavior.

A second line of reasoning relies on externalization. Cognitive processes are removed from the organism and placed in external stimuli. For example, people who believe they cannot avert potential dangers avoid such situations because they expect adverse consequences would befall them. In the process of externalization, the expectation is displaced by an external stimulus as the causal factor. The anticipatory cognitive control is relabeled as a preaversive stimulus exercising discriminative control over an avoidant repertoire. External stimuli carry the burden of explanation. The empirical evidence shows that human behavior is better predicted by anticipated outcomes than by actual outcomes.

The third strategy is the cognitive bypass operation. A causal sequence is depicted as one in which environmental stimuli causes the cognitive events, which in turn are linked to behavior. Since cognitions are simply products of external stimuli, cognition becomes a redundant link in the causal chain. You can bypass it and explain the behavior in terms of external stimuli.

A major problem with the cognitive bypass argument is that external stimuli are often poor predictors of thoughts and behavior. Behavior often is unaffected by its consequences. As a result, radical behaviorists now increasingly place the explanatory burden on the residue of past stimulus inputs.

Thoughts are not just conditioned products that are automatically triggered by external stimuli. There are creative and intentional aspects to human thought. I can readily generate several novel patterns of behavior, and choose to enact one of them. None of these would be replicas of past or present stimulus input. What we are dealing with here is the human capacity for intentionality and creative agency. I can generate a fanciful cognition in which merry hippopotamuses in chartreuse tuxedos are gracefully hang-gliding over lunar craters. That's a cognitive creation!

In disputing the causal role of thought, radical behaviorists depict cognitive events as disembodied mental states. They then invoke the dualism argument: How can an immaterial mind interact with a material body? In social cognitive theory, thought processes are brain processes. They are not immaterial essences floating above the brain. If one were to perform Bunge's hypothetical brain transplant, the donor's psychic life would accompany the brain to the host organism rather than stay behind with the donor.

The intriguing issue is not how do mind and body interact, because cognitive and cerebral terms refer to the same thing—brain processes. The challenging question is how can we be producers of thoughts that are novel, inventive, visionary, or completely fanciful. These issues concern the brain dynamics of cognitive generation. In addition to explaining how people create organized patterns of thought is the intriguing question of how they analyze the adequacy of their own thinking and correct it when it is judged to be faulty.

The fourth cognitive elimination strategy relies on an environmental implantation. Radical behaviorists contend that past stimulus inputs get implanted in the organism and behavior is inputs controlled by the stored implants. We are certainly influenced by what we make of our past experiences, but cognitive processes are not simply replicas of past stimulus inputs. Experiences are filtered through personal meanings and biases. People not only influence how they cognitively represent past events, but their memory of them as well. These processes involve the interpretive, creative, and generative nature of human thought rather than mechanically implanted stimuli.

EVANS: In conclusion, could you discuss the book you've most recently completed?

BANDURA: It bears the cosmic title, *Social Foundations of Thought and Action* (Bandura, 1986). In this book I analyze human motivation, thought, and action from a social cognitive perspective. The organizing theme is reciprocal determinism, which provides people with opportunities to exert some control over their destinies as well as sets limits of self-direction. New technologies are transforming the nature and scope of human influences, our social systems, and the way in which people live their lives. In this book I have tried to analyze human lives from a broader social perspective that transcends the arbitrary boundaries of academic disciplines. These interdisciplinary excursions turned out to be formidable tasks. To begin with a book of this scope in mind would require a touch of lunacy and high tolerance for self-inflicted toil. But if you start out innocently with a more circumscribed project in mind with fascinating dimensions, it can grow on you imperceptibly to huge proportions.

EVANS: Dr. Bandura, engaging in this discussion with you has been most delightful. Your enthusiasm is just marvelous. Thank you for your fine cooperation in this project, both in completing our filmed dialogues and this volume.

References

Ader, R., & Cohen, N. (1981). "Conditioned immunopharmacologic responses." In R. Ader (Ed.), *Psychoneuroimmunology* (pp. 281–319). New York: Academic Press.

Angell, M. (1985). Disease as a reflection of the psyche. *The New England Journal of Medicine, 312,* 1570–1572.

Ashton, P. T., & Webb, R. B. (1986). *Making a difference: Teachers' sense of efficacy and student achievement.* White Plains, NY: Longman.

Bandura, A. (1986). *Social foundations of thought and action: A social cognitive theory.* Englewood Cliffs, NJ: Prentice-Hall.

———. (1973). *Aggression: A social learning analysis.* Englewood Cliffs, NJ: Prentice-Hall.

———. (1969). *Principles of behavior modification.* New York: Holt, Rinehart & Winston.

Bandura, A., Cioffi, D. M., Taylor, C. B., & Brouillard, M. E. (1988). Perceived self-efficacy in coping with cognitive stressors and opioid activation. *Journal of Personality and Social Psychology, 55,* 479–488.

Bandura, A., Taylor, C. B., Williams, S. L., Millford, W. F., & Barchas, J. D. (1985). Catecholamine secretions and the function of perceived coping self-efficacy. *Journal of Consulting and Clinical Psychology, 53,* 406–414.

Bandura, A., & Schunk, D. H. (1981). Cultivating competence, self-efficacy and intrinsic interest through proximal self-motivation. *Journal of Personality and Social Psychology, 41*, 586–598.

Collins, J. L. (1982, March). *Self-efficacy and ability in achievement behavior.* Paper presented at the American Education Research Association, New York.

Comer, J. P. (1980). *School Power.* New York: Free Press.

Delgado, J. M. (1967). Social rank and radio-stimulated aggressiveness in monkeys. *Journal of Abnormal and Social Psychology, 47*, 309–315.

Evans, R. I. (1981). *Dialogue with Gordon Allport.* New York: Praeger.

————. (1981). *Dialogue with Erik Erikson.* New York: Praeger.

————. (1981). *Dialogue with Erich Fromm.* New York: Praeger.

————. (1981). *Dialogue with C. G. Jung.* New York: Praeger.

————. (1981). *Dialogue with Jean Piaget.* New York: Praeger.

————. (1981). *Dialogue with Carl Rogers.* New York: Praeger.

————. (1981). *Dialogue with B. F. Skinner.* New York: Praeger.

————. (1981). *Psychology and Arthur Miller.* New York: Praeger.

————. (1976). Smoking in children: Developing a social psychological strategy of deterrence. *Journal of Preventive Medicine, 5*(1), 122–127.

————. (1975). *Konrad Lorenz: The Man and His Ideas.* New York: Harcourt Brace Jovanovich, Inc.

Evans, R. I., Rozelle, R. M., Maxwell, S. E., Raines, B. E., Dill, C. A., Guthrie, T. J., Henderson, A. H., & Hill, P. C. (1981). Social modeling films to deter smoking in adolescents: Results of a three-year field investigation. *Journal of Applied Psychology, 66*(4), 399–414.

Evans, R. I., Rozelle, R. M., Mittelmark, M. B., Hansen, W. B., Bane, A. L., & Havis, J. (1978). Deterring the onset of smoking in children: Knowledge of immediate physiological effects and coping with peer pressure, media pressure, and parent modeling. *Journal of Applied Social Psychology, 8*, 126–135.

Fisher, Kathleen. (1983, August). 'Visual history' of psychology. *Monitor.*

Freud, S. (1937). "Die endliche und die unendliche Analyse", G. W., 16, 59. (80, 129, 138) ["Analysis Terminable and Interminable"], C. P., 5, 316; Standard Ed., 23.

————. (1933). *New introductory lectures on psychoanalysis*. New York: Morton.

Garcia, J., & Koelling, R. A. (1966). Relation of cue to consequence and avoidance learning. *Psychonomic Science, 4*, 123–124.

Gibson, S., & Dembo, M. H. (1984). Teacher efficacy: A construct validation. *Journal of Educational Psychology, 76*, 569–582.

Joyce, James, Introduction by Padraic Colum (1954). *Dubliners*. New York: The Modern Library.

Kiecolt-Glaser, J. K., & Glaser, R. (in press). "Behavioral influences on immune function: Evidence for the interplay between stress and health." In T. Field, P. M. McCabe, & N. Schneiderman (Eds.), *Stress and coping across development* (Vol. 2). Hillsdale, NJ: Lawrence Erlbaum.

Kiecolt-Glaser, J. K., Glaser, R., Strain, E. C., Stout, J. C., Tarr, K. L., Holliday, J. E., & Speicher, C. E. (1986). Modulation of cellular immunity in medical students. *Journal of Behavioral Medicine, 9*, 5–21.

Kiecolt-Glaser, J. K., Glaser, R., Williger, D., Stout, J., Messick, G., Sheppard, S., Ricker, D., Romisher, S. C., Birner, W., Bonnell, G., & Donnerberg, R. (1985). Psychosocial enhancement of immunocompetence in a geriatric population. *Health Psychology, 4*, 25–41.

Lorenz, K. (1966). *On aggression*. New York: Harcourt Brace Jovanovich.

Maier, S. F., Landenslager, M. L., & Ryan, S. M. (1985). "Stressor controllability, immune function, and endogenous opiates." In F. R. Brush & J. B. Wvermier (Eds.), *Affect, conditioning and cognition: Essays on the determinants of behavior* (pp. 183–201). Hillsdale, NJ: Lawrence Erlbaum.

Milgram, S. (1974). *Obedience to authority: An experimental view*. New York: Harper & Row.

Miller, N. E., & Dollard, J. (1941). *Social learning and imitation*. New Haven: Yale University Press.

Rosenthal, R., & Rubin, D. B. (1980). Further issues in summarizing 345 studies of interpersonal expectancy effects. *Behavioral and Brain Sciences, 3*, 475–476.

————. (1978). Interpersonal expectancy effects: The first 345 studies. *Behavioral and Brain Sciences, 1*, 377–415.

Rosenthal, R., & Jacobsen, L. (1968) *Pygmalion in the classroom*. New York: Holt, Rinehart & Winston.

Sarason, I. G., Sarason, B. R. & Pierce, G. R. (1988). "Social support, personality, and health." In S. Maes, C. D. Spielberger, P. B. Defares, & I. G. Sarason (Eds.), *Topics in health psychology*. New York: John Wiley and Sons.

Schunk, D. H. (1987). Peer models and children's behavioral change. *Review of Educational Research, 57,* 149–174.

————. (1984). Self-efficacy perspective on achievement behavior. *Educational Psychologist, 19,* 48–58.

Simonton, O. C., Matthews, S., & Simonton, S. (1982). Cancer and stress. Counselling the cancer patient. *Medical Journal of Australia,* June, 679–683.

Taylor, C. B., Bandura, A., Ewart, C. K., Miller, N. H., & DeBusk, R. N. (1985). Exercise testing to enhance wives' confidence in their husbands' cardiac capabilities soon after clinically uncomplicated acute myocardial infarction. *American Journal of Cardiology, 55,* 635–638.

Watters, J. K. (1987). *Preventing human immunodeficiency virus contagion among intravenous drug users: The impact of street-based education on risk-behavior.* Unpublished manuscript.

White, J. (1982). *Rejection.* Reading, MA: Addison-Wesley.

Wiedenfeld, S. A., O'Leary, A., Bandura, A., & Brown, S. *Impact of perceived self-efficacy in coping with stressors on immune function.* Submitted for publication.

Williams, R. B., Jr. (1987). Refining the Type A hypothesis: Emergence of the hostility complex. *American Journal of Cardiology, 60*(18), 27J–32J.

Bibliography: Works of Albert Bandura

With L. E. Parker. *The determinants and effects of perceived collective effi- cacy.* In preparation.

With S. A. Wiedenfeld, A. O'Leary, & S. Brown, S. Levine & K. Raska. *Impact of perceived self-efficacy in coping with stressors on immune function.*

With E. M. Ozer. *Mechanisms governing empowerment effects: A self-effi- cacy analysis.* Submitted for publication.

Human agency in social cognitive theory. American Psychologist. In press.

With W. R. Carroll. *The joint operation of representational and transfor- mational mechanisms in observational learning.*

Regulation of cognitive processes through perceived self-efficacy. *De- velopmental Psychology.* In press.

Reflections on nonability determinants of competence. In J. Kolligian, Jr., & R. J. Sternberg (Eds.), *Competence considered: Perceptions of competence and incompetence across the lifespan.* New Haven, CT: Yale University Press. In press.

A social cognitive theory of action. In J. P. Forgas & M. J. Innes (Eds.), *Social psychology. Vol. 1. Proceedings of the XXIV International Con- gress of Psychology.* North Holland: Elsevier, 1989. In press.

Selective activation and disengagement of moral control. *Journal of So- cial Issues.* In press.

Perceived self-efficacy in the exercise of personal agency. *Psychologist*. In press.

The changing icons of personality psychology. In J. H. Cantor (Ed.), *Psychology at Iowa: Centennial Essays*. Hillsdale, NJ: Erlbaum, in press.

Psychological aspects of prognostic judgments. In R. W. Evans, D. S. Baskin, & F. M. Yatsu (Eds.), *Prognosis in neurological disease*. New York: Oxford University Press, in press.

Self-efficacy mechanism in physiological activation and health-promoting behavior. In J. Madden, IV, S. Matthysse, & J. Barchas (Eds.), *Adaptation, learning and affect*. New York: Raven Press, 1989. In press.

Social cognitive theory and social referencing. In S. Feinman (Ed.), *Social referencing and social construction of reality*. New York: Plenum, 1989.

Impact of perceived self-efficacy on adolescent life paths. In R. M. Lerner, A. C. Peterson, & J. Brooks-Gunn (Eds.), *The encyclopedia of adolescence*. New York: Plenum. In press.

With W. R. Carroll. Representational guidance of action production in observational learning: A causal analysis. *Journal of Motor Behavior*. In press.

Perceived self-efficacy in the exercise of control over AIDS infection. In S. Blumenthal & A. Eichler (Eds.), *Women and AIDS*. In press.

Social cognitive theory of moral thought and action. In W. M. Kurtines & J. L. Gewirtz (Eds.), *Moral behavior and development: Advances in theory, research and applications* (Vol. 1) pp. 71–129. Hillsdale, NJ: Erlbaum. In press.

Self-regulation of motivation and action through internal standards and goal systems. In L. A. Pervin (Ed.), *Goals concepts in personality and social psychology*. Hillsdale, NJ: Erlbaum, 1989, pp. 19–85.

Social cognitive theory of mass communication. In V. Groebel & P. Winterhoff (Eds.), *Empirische Medienpsychologie*. München: Psychologie Verlags Union, 1989.

With R. E. Wood. Effect of perceived controllability and performance standards on self-regulation of complex decision making. *Journal of Personality and Social Psychology*. In press.

With R. E. Wood. Social cognitive theory of organizational management. *Academy of Management Review*, 14. In press.

With R. E. Wood. Impact of conceptions of ability on self-regulatory mechanisms and complex decision making. *Journal of Personality and Social Psychology*, 56, 1989, 407–415.

With R. E. Wood & T. Bailey. Mechanisms governing motivation and productivity in complex decision making environments. *Organizational Behavior and Human Decision Processes*. In press.

Social cognitive theory. In E. Barnouw (Ed.), *International encyclopedia of communications*. New York: Oxford University Press. In press.

Mechanisms of moral disengagement in terrorism. In W. Reich (Ed.), *The Psychology of terrorism: Behaviors, world-views, states of mind*. Cambridge: Cambridge University Press. In press.

Perceived self-efficacy: Exercise of control through self-belief. In J. P. Dauwalder, M. Perrez, & V. Hobi (Eds.), *Annual series of European research in behavior therapy*, (Vol. 2). Lisse (NL): Swets & Zeitlinger, 1988, pp. 27–59.

Self-efficacy conception of anxiety. *Anxiety Research*, 1988, *I*, 77–98.

Self-regulation of motivation and action through goal systems. In V. Hamilton, G. H. Bower, & N. H. Frijda (Eds.), *Cognitive perspectives on emotion and motivation*. Dordrecht: Kluwer Academic Publishers, 1988, pp. 37–61.

Social cognitive theory. In R. Vasta (Ed.), *Annals of child development: Vol. 6. Six theories of child development*. Greenwich, CT : JAI Press, 1988, pp. 1–60.

With D. M. Cioffi, C. B. Taylor, & M. E. Brouillard. Perceived self-efficacy in coping with cognitive stressors and opioid activation. *Journal of Personality and Social Psychology*, 1988, 55 479–488.

With A. O'Leary, C. B. Taylor, J. Gauthier, & D. Gossard. Perceived self-efficacy and pain control: Opioid and nonopioid mechanisms. *Journal of Personality and Social Psychology*, 1987, *63*, 563–571.

With W. R. Carroll. Translating cognition into action: The role of visual guidance in observational learning. *Journal of Motor Behavior*, 1987, *19*, 385–398.

The explanatory and predictive scope of self-efficacy theory. *Journal of Clinical and Social Psychology*, 1986, *4*, 359–373.

From thought to action: Mechanisms of personal agency. *New Zealand Journal of Psychology*, 1986, *15*, 1–17.

Social foundations of thought and action: A social cognitive theory. Englewood Cliffs, NJ: Prentice-Hall, 1986. (Spanish edition, *Pensa-*

miento y accion: Fundamentos sociales, Maria Zaplana [Trans.], Barcelona: Martinez Roca, 1987.)

With D. Cervone. Differential engagement of self-reactive influences in cognitive motivation. *Organizational Behavior and Human Decision Processes,* 1986, *38,* 92–113.

With W. R. Carroll. Role of timing of visual monitoring and motor rehearsal in observational learning of action patterns. *Journal of Motor Behavior,* 1985, *17,* 269–281.

With C. B. Taylor, C. K. Ewart, N. H. Miller, & R. N. DeBusk. Exercise testing to enhance wives' confidence in their husbands' cardiac capability soon after clinically uncomplicated acute myocardial infarction. *American Journal of Cardiology,* 1985, *55,* 635–638.

With C. B. Taylor, S. L. Williams, I. N. Millord, & J. D. Barchas. Catecholamine secretions and the function of perceived coping self-efficacy. *Journal of Consulting and Clinical Psychology,* 1985, *53,* 406–414.

Reciprocal determinism. In S. Sukemune (Ed.), *Advances in social learning theory. Bandura in Japan.* Tokyo: Kaneko-shoho, 1985.

Explorations in self-efficacy. In S. Sukemune (Ed.), *Advances in social learning theory. Bandura in Japan.* Tokyo: Kaneko-shoho, 1985.

Observational learning. In S. Sukemune (Ed.), *Advances in social learning theory. Bandura in Japan.* Tokyo: Kaneko-shoho, 1985.

Model of causality in social learning theory. In S. Sukemune (Ed.), *Advances in social learning theory. Bandura in Japan.* Tokyo: Kaneko-shoho, 1985. (Reprinted in, M. J. Mahoney & A. Freeman [Eds.], *Cognition and psychotherapy.* New York: Plenum, 1985.)

With K. Bussey. Influence of gender constancy and social power on sex-linked modeling. *Journal of Personality and Social Psychology,* 1984, *47,* 1292–1302.

Representing personal determinants in causal structures. *Psychological Review,* 1984, *91,* 508–511.

Recycling misconceptions of perceived self-efficacy. *Cognitive Therapy and Research,* 1984, *8,* 231–255.

With D. Cervone. Self-evaluative and self-efficacy mechanisms governing the motivational effects of goal systems. *Journal of Personality and Social Psychology,* 1983, *45,* 1017–1028.

Self-efficacy determinants of anticipated fears and calamities. *Journal of Personality and Social Psychology,* 1983, *45* 464–469.

Temporal dynamics and decomposition of reciprocal determinism. *Psychological Review*, 1982, *90*, 166–170.

Self-efficacy determinants of anticipated fears and calamities. *Journal of Behavior Therapy and Experimental Psychiatry*, 1982, *13*, 195–199.

With W. R. Carroll. The role of visual monitoring in observational learning of action patterns: Making the unobservable observable. *Journal of Motor Behavior*, 1982, *14*, 153–167.

With M. J. Telch, P. Vinciguerra, A. Agras, & A. L. Stout. Social demand for consistency and congruence between self-efficacy and performance. *Behavior Therapy*, 1982, *13*, 694–701.

With L. Reese & N. E. Adams. Microanalysis of action and fear arousal as a function of differential levels of perceived self-efficacy. *Journal of Personality and Social Psychology*, 1982, *43*, 5–21.

The psychology of chance encounters and life paths. *American Psychologist*, 1982, *37*, 747–755.

Self-efficacy mechanism in human agency. *American Psychologist*, 1982, *37*, 122–147.

The self and mechanisms of agency. In J. Suls (Ed.), *Psychological perspectives on the self* (Vol. 1). Hillsdale, NJ: Erlbaum, 1982.

With D. H. Schunk. Cultivating competence, self-efficacy, and intrinsic interest through proximal self-motivation. *Journal of Personality and Social Psychology*, 1981, *41*, 586–598.

In search of pure unidirectional determinants. *Behavior Therapy*, 1981, *12*, 30–40.

Self-referent thought: A developmental analysis of self-efficacy. In J. H. Flavell & L. Ross (Eds.), *Social cognitive development: Frontiers and possible futures*. Cambridge: Cambridge University Press, 1981. (Reprinted in, H. J. Walter [Ed.], *Gestalt Theory*, 1980, *2*, 147–174.)

Gauging the relationship between self-efficacy judgment and action. *Cognitive Therapy and Research*, 1980, *4*, 263–268.

With N. E. Adams, A. B. Hardy, & G. N. Howells. Tests of the generality of self-efficacy theory. *Cognitive Therapy and Research*, 1980, *4*, 39–66.

On ecumenism in research perspectives. *Cognitive Therapy and Research*, 1979, *3*, 245–248.

Self-referent mechanisms in social learning theory. *American Psychologist*, 1979, *34*, 439–441.

Psychological mechanisms of aggression. In M. VonGranach, K. Foppa, W. LePenies, & D. Ploog (Eds.), *Human ethology: Claims and limits of a new discipline.* Cambridge: Cambridge University Press, 1979. (Reprinted in, G. Gerbner [Ed.], *Journal of Communication,* 1988, *28*[3], 12–29; H. Toch [Ed.], *Psychology of crime and criminal justice.* New York: Holt, Rinehart & Winston, 1979; R. G. Geen & E. Donnerstein [Eds.], *Aggression: Theoretical and empirical reviews.* New York: Academic Press, 1983.)

On paradigms and recycled ideologies. *Cognitive Therapy and Research,* 1978, *2,* 79–103. (Reprinted in S. Rachman [Ed.], *Contributions to medical psychology,* (Vol. 3). New York: Pergamon Press, 1984, 225–245.)

With T. L. Rosenthal. Psychological modeling: Theory and practice. In S. L. Garfield & A. E. Bergin (Eds.), *Handbook of psychotherapy and behavior change* (2nd ed.). New York: Wiley, 1978.

On distinguishing between logical and empirical verification. *Scandinavian Journal of Psychology,* 1978, *19,* 97–99.

Reflections on self-efficacy. In S. Rachman (Ed.), *Advances in behavior research and therapy* (Vol. 1). Oxford: Pergamon Press, 1978. (Reprinted in, C. M. Franks & G. T. Wilson [Eds.], *Annual review of behavior therapy theory and practice* [Vol. 7]. New York: Brunner/Mazel, 1980.)

The self system in reciprocal determinism. *American Psychologist,* 1978, *33,* 344–358. (Reprinted in, V. F. Guidano & M. A. Reda [Eds.], *Cognitivismo e psicoterapia.* Milan, Italy: Franco Angeli, 1981.).

Self-efficacy: Toward a unifying theory of behavioral change. *Psychological Review,* 1977, *84,* 191–215. (Reprinted in, C. M. Franks & G. T. Willson [Eds.], *Annual review of behavior therapy theory and practice* [Vol. 6]. New York: Brunner/Mazel, 1978; S. Rachman [Ed.], *Advances in behavior research and therapy* [*Vol. 1*]. *Oxford: Pergamon Press, 1978; M. Rosenberg & H. B. Kaplan* [Eds.], *Social psychology of the self-concept.* Arlington Heights, IL: Harlan Davidson, 1982.)

With N. E. Adams. Analysis of self-efficacy theory of behavioral change. *Cognitive Therapy and Research,* 1977, *1,* 287–308.

With N. E. Adams & J. Beyer. Cognitive processes mediating behavioral change. *Journal of Personality and Social Psychology,* 1977, *35,* 125–139.

With K. M. Simon. The role of proximal intentions in self-regulation of refractory behavior. *Cognitive Therapy and Research*, 1977, 1, 177–193. (Reprinted in, C. M. Franks & G. T. Wilson [Eds.], *Annual review of behavior therapy theory and practice* [Vol. 6]. New York: Brunner/Mazel, 1978.)

Self-reinforcement: The power of positive personal control. In P. G. Zimbardo & F. L. Ruch, *Psychology and life* (9th ed.). Glenview, IL: Scott, Foresman, 1977.

Social learning theory. In B. B. Wolman & L. R. Pomroy (Eds.), *International encyclopedia of psychiatry, psychology, psychoanalysis, and neurology* (Vol. 10). New York: Van Nostrand Reinhold, 1977.

Social learning theory. Englewood Cliffs, NJ: Prentice-Hall, 1977. (French edition, *L'apprentissage social*, J. A. Rondal [Trans.], Bruxelles: Pierre Mardaga, 1980; German edition, *Sozial-kognitive Lerntheorie*, H. Kober [Trans.], Stuttgart: Klett-Cotta, 1979; Japanese edition, *Shakaiteki gakushu riron*, K. Harano [Trans.], Tokyo: Kaneko-shoho, 1979; Spanish edition, *Teoria del aprendizaje social*, A. Riviere [Trans.], Madrid: Espana-Calpe, 1982.)

Observational learning. *Proceedings of the XXIst International Congress of Psychology*, Paris, France, 1976. (Abstract).

Social learning perspective on behavior change. In A. Burton (Ed.), *What makes behavior change possible?* New York: Brunner/Mazel, 1976.

Effecting change through participant modeling. In J. D. Krumboltz & C. E. Thoresen (Eds.), *Counseling methods.* New York: Holt, Rinehart & Winston, 1976.

New perspectives on violence. In V. C. Vaughan, III & T. B. Brazelton (Eds.), *The family.* Chicago: Year Book Medical Publishers, 1976.

With M. J. Mahoney & S. J. Dirks. Discriminative activation and maintenance of contingent self-reinforcement. *Behaviour Research and Therapy*, 1976, 14, 1–6.

Social learning analysis of aggression. In E. Ribes-Inesta & A. Bandura (Eds.), *Analysis of delinquency and aggression.* Hillsdale, NJ: Erlbaum, 1976.

With E. Ribes-Inesta (Eds.), *Analysis of delinquency and aggression.* Hillsdale, NJ: Erlbaum, 1976.

Self-reinforcement: Theoretical and methodological considerations. *Behaviorism*, 1976, 4, 135–155. (Reprinted in, C. M. Franks & G. T.

Wilson [Eds.], *Annual review of behavior therapy theory and practice* [Vol. 5]. New York: Brunner/Mazel, 1977.)

The ethics and social purposes of behavior modification. In C. M. Franks & G. T. Wilson (Eds.), *Annual review of behavior therapy theory and practice* (Vol. 3). New York: Brunner/Mazel, 1975.

With R. W. Jeffery & E. Gajdos. Generalizing change through participant modeling with self-directed mastery. *Behaviour Research and Therapy*, 1975, *13*, 141–152. (Reprinted in, C. M. Franks & G. T. Wilson [Eds.], *Annual review of behavior therapy theory and practice* [Vol. 4.]. New York: Brunner/Mazel, 1976.)

With B. Underwood & M. E. Fromson. Disinhibition of aggression through diffusion of responsibility and dehumanization of victims. *Journal of Research in Personality*, 1975, *9*, 253–269. (Reprinted in, P. G. Zimbardo & C. Maslach [Eds.], *Psychology for our times: Readings* [2nd ed.]. Glenview, IL: Scott, Foresman, 1977.)

With R. W. Jeffery & D. L. Bachicha. Analysis of memory codes and cumulative rehearsal in observational learning. *Journal of Research in Personality*, 1974, *7*, 295–305.

With M. J. Mahoney, S. J. Dirks, & C. L. Wright. Relative preference for external and self-controlled reinforcement in monkeys. *Behaviour Research and Therapy*, 1974, *12*, 157–163.

With M. J. Mahoney. Maintenance and transfer of self-reinforcement functions. *Behaviour Research and Therapy*, 1974, *12*, 89–97.

The process and practice of participant modeling treatment. In J. H. Cullen (Ed.), *Experimental behaviour: A basis for the study of mental disturbance*. Dublin: Irish University Press, 1974.

With R. W. Jeffery & C. L. Wright. Efficacy of participant modeling as a function of response induction aids. *Journal of Abnormal Psychology*, 1974, *83*, 56–64. (Reprinted in, C. M. Franks & G. T. Wilson [Eds.], *Annual review of behavior therapy theory and practice* [Vol. 3]. New York: Brunner/Mazel, 1975).

The case of the mistaken dependent variable. *Journal of Abnormal Psychology*, 1974, *83*, 301–303.

Behavior theory and the models of man. *American Psychologist*, 1974, *29*, 859–869. (Reprinted in, C. M. Franks & G. T. Wilson [Eds.], *Annual review of behavior therapy theory and practice* [Vol. 4]. New York: Brunner/Mazel, 1976; E. P. Hollander & R. G. Hunt [Eds.], *Current perspectives in social psychology* [4th ed.]. Oxford: Oxford

University Press, 1976; A. Wandersman, P. J. Poppen, & D. F. Ricks [Eds.], *Humanism and behaviorism: Dialogue and growth.* Elmsford, NY: Pergamon Press, 1976; D. P. Kimble [Ed.], *Contrast and controversy in modern psychology.* Santa Monica, CA: Goodyear, 1977; E. A. Southwell & M. Merbaum [Eds.], *Personality: Readings in theory and research* [3rd ed.]. Monterey, CA: Brooks/Cole, 1978; T. Millon [Ed.], *Theories of personality and pathology* [3rd ed.]. New York: Holt, Rinehart and Winston.

Institutionally sanctioned violence. *Journal of Clinical Child Psychology,* 1973, *2,* 23–24. (Reprinted in, M. Wertheimer & L. Rappoport [Eds.], *Psychology and the problems of today.* Glenview, IL: Scott, Foresman, 1978).

Social learning theory of aggression. In J. F. Knutson (Ed.), *The control of aggression: Implications from basic research.* Chicago: Aldine, 1973. (Reprinted in E. P. Hollander & R. G. Hunt [Eds.], *Current perspectives in social psychology* [4th ed.]. Oxford: Oxford University Press, 1976; I. L. Kutash, S. B. Kutash, & L. B. Schlesinger [Eds.], *Violence: Perspectives on murder and aggression.* San Francisco: Jossey-Bass, 1978.

With P. G. Barab. Processes governing disinhibitory effects through symbolic modeling. *Journal of Abnormal Psychology,* 1973, *82,* 1–9.

With R. W. Jeffery. Role of symbolic coding and rehearsal processes in observational learning. *Journal of Personality and Social Psychology,* 1973, *26,* 122–130.

Aggression: A social learning analysis. Englewood Cliffs, NJ: Prentice-Hall, 1973. (German edition, *Aggression: Eine sozial-lerntheoretische Analyse,* U. Olligschlagear [Trans.], Stuttgart: Klett-Cotta, 1979.)

With M. J. Mahoney. Self-reinforcement in pigeons. *Learning and Motivation,* 1972, *3,* 293–303.

Socialization. In *Lexikon der Psychologie.* Band III. Freiburg im Breisgau: Herder, 1972.

Social learning theory. New York: General Learning Press, 1971. (Japanese edition, *Ningenkodo no keisei to jikoseigyo,* K. Harano & O. Fukushima [Trans.], Tokyo: Kaneko-shoho, 1974; Reprinted in, J. T. Spence, R. C. Carson, & J. W. Thibaut [Eds.], *Behavioral approaches to therapy.* Morristown, NJ: General Learning Press, 1976.)

Analysis of modeling processes. In A. Bandura (Ed.), *Psychological modeling: Conflicting theories.* Chicago: Aldin-Atherton, 1971, (Reprinted in, E. M. Hetherington & R. D. Parker [Eds.], *Contemporary readings in child psychology.* New York: McGraw-Hill, 1977.)

(Ed.). *Psychological modeling: Conflicting theories.* New York: Aldine-Atherton, 1971. (German edition, *Lernen am Modell: Ansätze zu einer sozial-kognitiven Lerntheorie,* H. Kober, [Trans.], Stuttgart: Klett-Cotta, 1976; Japanese edition, *Moderingu no shinrigaku,* K. Harano & O. Fukushima [Trans.], Tokyo: Kaneko-shoho, 1975.)

With P. G. Barab. Conditions governing nonreinforced imitation. *Developmental Psychology,* 1971, 5, 244–255.

Psychotherapy based upon modeling principles. In A. E. Bergin & S. L. Garfield (Eds.), *Handbook of psychotherapy and behavior change.* New York: Wiley, 1971.

Behavior therapy from a social learning perspective. *Proceedings of the XIXth International Congress of Psychology.* London, England, 1971.

Vicarious and self-reinforcement processes. In R. Glaser (Ed.), *The nature of reinforcement.* New York: Academic Press, 1971. (Reprinted in, M. J. Mahoney & C. E. Thoresen [Eds.], *Self control: Power to the person.* Monterey, CA: Brooks/Cole, 1974).

Modeling theory: Some traditions, trends and disputes. In W. S. Sahakian (Ed.), *Psychology of learning: Systems, models, and theories.* Chicago: Markham, 1970. (Reprinted in, R. D. Parke [Ed.], *Recent trends in social learning theory.* New York: Academic Press, 1972.)

With E. B. Blanchard & B. Ritter. Relative efficacy of desensitization and modeling approaches for inducing behavioral, affective, and attitudinal changes. *Journal of Personality and Social Psychology,* 1969, 13, 173–199. (Reprinted in, J. Willis & D. Giles [Eds.], *Great experiments in behavior modification.* Indianapolis, IN: Hackett, 1976; W. L. Mikulas [Ed.], *Psychology of learning: Readings.* Chicago: Nelson-Hall, 1977.)

Social learning of moral judgments. *Journal of Personality and Social Psychology.* 1969, 11, 275–279.

Principles of behavior modification. New York: Holt, Rinehart & Winston, 1969. (Portuguese edition, *Modificacao do comportamento,* E. Nick [Trans.], Rio de Janeiro: Editora Interamericana, 1979; Spanish edition, *Principios de modificacion de conducta*, J. Almaraz [Trans.], Salamanca: Ediciones Sigueme, 1983.)

Social-learning theory of identificatory processes. In D. A. Goslin (Ed.), *Handbook of socialization theory and research*. Chicago: Rand McNally, 1969.

Modeling approaches to the modification of phobic disorders. In R. Porter (Ed.), *The role of learning in psychotherapy: Ciba Foundation Symposium*. London: Churchill, 1968. (Reprinted in, W. S. Sahakian [Ed.], *Psychopathology today: Experimentation, theory, and research*. Itasca, IL: Peacock, 1970.)

On empirical disconfirmations of equivocal deductions with insufficient data. *Journal of Consulting and Clinical Psychology*, 1968, *32*, 247–249.

With F. L. Menlove. Factors determining vicarious extinction through symbolic modeling. *Journal of Personality and Social Psychology*, 1968, *8*, 99–108. (Reprinted in, R. M. Liebert & R. A. Baron [Eds.], *Human social behavior: A contemporary view*. Homewood, IL: Dorsey Press, 1971; H. Mischel & W. Mischel [Eds.], *Readings in personality*. New York: Holt, Rinehart & Winston, 1973; A. A. Harrison [Ed.], *Explorations in psychology*. Monterey, CA: Brooks/Cole, 1974.)

A social learning interpretation of psychological dysfunctions. In P. London & D. L. Rosenhan (Eds.), *Foundations of abnormal psychology*. New York: Holt, Rinehart & Winston, 1968.

Reinforcement therapy: An antidote for therapeutic pessimism. (Review of Reinforcement therapy by O. I. Lovaas). *Contemporary Psychology*, 1968, *13*, 36–39.

Imitation. In D. L. Sills (Ed.), *International encyclopedia of the social sciences* (Vol. 7). New York: Macmillan, 1968.

The role of modeling processes in personality development. In W. W. Hartup & N. L. Smothergill (Eds.), *The young child*. Washington: National Association for the Education of Young Children, 1967. (Reprinted in, D. M. Gelfand [Ed.], *Readings in child development and behavior modification*. Belmont, CA: Brooks/Cole, 1969; N. H. Pronko [Ed.], *Panorama of psychology*. Belmont, CA: Brooks/Cole, 1969; J. M. Foley, R. Lockhart, & D. Messick [Eds.], *Contemporary readings in psychology*. New York: Harper & Row, 1970; S. Cohen [Ed.], *Child development: A study of growth processes*. Itasca, IL: Peacock, 1971; R. M. Stutz, W. N. Dember, & J. J.

Jenkins [Eds.], *Exploring behavior and experience: Readings in general psychology*. Englewood Cliffs, NJ: Prentice-Hall, 1971; C. S. Lavatelli & F. Stendler [Eds.], *Readings in child behavior and development* [3rd ed.]. New York: Harcourt, Brace Jovanovich, 1972; R. E. Silverman [Ed.], *Readings for psychology*. New York: Appleton-Century-Crofts, 1972; A. M. Sandowsky [Ed.], *Child and adolescent development*. New York: Free Press, 1973; D. M. Gelfand [Ed.], *Social learning in childhood: Readings in theory and application*. Monterey, CA: Brooks/Cole, 1975.)

With B. Perloff. Relative efficacy of self-monitored and externally-imposed reinforcement systems. *Journal of Personality and Social Psychology*, 1967, *7*, 111–116. (Reprinted in, I. J. Gordon [Ed.], *Readings in research in developmental psychology*. Glenview, IL: Scott, Foresman, 1971; E. McGinnies & C. B. Ferster [Eds.], *The reinforcement of social behavior*. Boston: Houghton Mifflin, 1971; K. D. O'Leary & S. G. O'Leary [Eds.], *Classroom management: The successful use of behavior modification*. Oxford: Pergamon Press, 1972; M. R. Goldfried & M. Merbaum [Eds.], *Behavior change through self-control*. New York: Holt, Rinehart & Winston, 1973).

With J. E. Grusec & F. L. Menlove. Vicarious extinction of avoidance bahavior. *Journal of Personality and Social Psychology*, 1967, *5*, 16–23. (Reprinted in, B. L. Kintz & J. L. Bruning [Eds.], *Research in psychology*. Glenview, IL: Scott, Foresman, 1969; I. G. Sarason [Ed.], *Contemporary research in personality*. Princeton: Van Nostrand, 1969; P. H. Mussen, J. J. Conger, & J. Kagan [Eds.], *Readings in child development and personality* [2nd ed.]. New York: Harper & Row, 1970; E. McGinnies & C. B. Ferster [Eds.], *The reinforcement of social behavior*. Boston: Houghton Mifflin, 1971; R. S. Browne, H. E. Freeman, C. V. Hamilton, J. Kagan, & A. K. Romney [Eds.], *The social scene: A contemporary view of the social sciences*. Cambridge, MA: Winthrop, 1972; K. D. O'Leary & S. G. O'Leary [Eds.], *Classroom management: The successful use of behavior modification*. Oxford: Pergamon Press, 1972; B. Ashem & E. G. Poser [Eds.], *Adaptive learning: Behavior modification with children*. Elmsford, NY: Pergamon Press, 1973; O. I. Lovaas & B. D. Bucher [Eds.], *Perspectives in behavior modification with deviant children*. Englewood Cliffs, NJ: Prentice-Hall, 1974; P. H. Mussen, J. J. Conger, & J. Kagan [Eds.], *Basic and contemporary issues in developmental psychology*. New York: Harper & Row, 1975.

With J. E. Grusec & F. L. Menlove. Some social determinants of self-monitoring reinforcement systems. *Journal of Personality and Social Psychology*, 1967, *5*, 449–455.

Behavioral psychotherapy. *Scientific American*, 1967, *216*(3), 78–86. (Reprinted in, R. C. Atkinson [Ed.], *Contemporary psychology*. San Francisco: Freeman, 1975; R. C. Atkinson [Ed.], *Psychology in progress*. San Francisco: Freeman, 1975; R. L. Atkinson & R. C. Atkinson [Eds.], *Mind and behavior: Readings from Scientific American*. San Francisco: Freeman, 1980.)

With T. L. Rosenthal. Vicarious classical conditioning as a function of arousal level. *Journal of Personality and Social Psychology*, 1966, *3*, 373–382.

With M. B. Harris. Modification of syntactic style. *Journal of Experimental Child Psychology*, 1966, *4*, 341–352. (Reprinted in, H. Munsinger [Ed.], *Readings in fundamentals of child psychology*. New York: Holt, Rinehart & Winston, 1971; M. B. Harris [Ed.], *Classroom use of behavior modification*. Columbus, OH: Merrill, 1972.)

With J. E. Grusec & F. L. Menlove. Observational learning as a function of symbolization and incentive set. *Child Development*, 1966, *37*, 499–506. (Reprinted in, R. D. Parke [Ed.], *Readings in social development*. New York: Holt, Rinehart & Winston, 1969.

Role of vicarious learning in personality development. *Proceedings of the XVIIIth International Congress of Psychology: Social factors in the development of personality*. Moscow, USSR, 1966.

With W. Mischel. Modification of self-imposed delay of reward through exposure to live and symbolic models. *Journal of Personality and Social Psychology*, 1965, *2*, 698–705. (Reprinted in, J. F. Rosenblith & W. Allinsmith [Eds.], *The causes of behavior*. II. Boston: Allyn & Bacon, 1966.)

Influence of models' reinforcement contingencies on the acquisition of imitative responses. *Journal of Personality and Social Psychology*, 1965, *1*, 589–595. (Reprinted in, R. D. Parke [Ed.], *Readings in social development*. New York: Holt, Rinehart & Winston, 1969; A. N. Doob & D. Regan [Eds.], *Readings in experimental social psychology*. New York: Appleton-Century-Crofts, 1971; E. McGinnies & C. B. Ferster [Eds.], *The reinforcement of social behavior*. Boston: Houghton Mifflin, 1971; H. J. Vetter & B. D. Smith [Eds.], *Personality theory: A source book*. New York: Appleton-Century-Crofts, 1971; B. Kleinmuntz [Ed.], *Readings in the essentials of abnormal psychology*. New York: Harper & Row, 1974. M. Coxrage [Ed.], *Selected readings in developmental psychology*. Ontario, Canada: Broadview Press, 1988).

Behavioral modification through modeling procedures. In L. Krasner & L. P. Ullmann (Eds.), *Research in behavior modification*. New York: Holt, Rinehart & Winston, 1965.

Vicarious processes: A case of no-trial learning. In L. Berkowitz (Ed.), *Advances in experimental social psychology* (Vol. 2). New York: Academic Press, 1965.

With C. J. Kupers. Transmission of patterns of self-reinforcement through modeling. *Journal of Abnormal and Social Psychology*, 1964, *69*, 1–9. (Reprinted in, E. P. Torrance & W. F. White [Eds.], *Issues and advances in educational psychology*. Itasca, IL: Peacock, 1969; H. J. Vetter & B. D. Smith [Eds.], *Personality theory: A source book*. New York: Appleton-Century-Crofts, 1971; K. D. O'Leary & S. G. O'Leary [Eds.], *Classroom management: The successful use of behavior modification*. Oxford: Pergamon Press, 1972; M. R. Goldfried & M. Merbaum [Eds.], *Behavior change through self-control*. New York: Holt, Rinehart & Winston, 1973.)

The stormy decade: Fact or fiction? *Psychology in the Schools*, 1964, *1*, 224–231. (Reprinted in, R. E. Grinder [Ed.], *Studies in adolescence: A book of readings in adolescent development*. II. New York: Macmillan, 1969; D. Rogers [Ed.], *Issues in adolescent psychology*. New York: Appleton-Century-Crofts, 1969; R. E. Muuss [Ed.], *Adolescent behavior and society: A book of readings*. New York: Random House, 1971, [2nd ed.], 1975; H. D. Thornburg [Ed.], *Contemporary adolescence: Readings*. Monterey, CA: Brooks/Cole, 1971.)

With R. H. Walters. *Social learning and personality development*. New York: Holt, Rinehart & Winston, 1963. (Spanish edition, *Aprendizaje social y desarrollo de la personalidad*, de Angel Riviere [Trans.], Madrid: Alianza Editorial, 1974.)

With R. H. Walters. Aggression. In *Child Psychology: The Sixty-second Yearbook of the National Society for the Study of Education, Part I*. Chicago: The National Society for the Study of Education, 1963.

With D. Ross & S. A. Ross. Vicarious reinforcement and imitative learning. *Journal of Abnormal and Social Psychology*, 1963, *67*, 601–607. (Reprinted in, A. W. Staats [Ed.], *Human learning*. New York: Holt, Rinehart & Winston, 1964; D. M. Gelfand [Ed.], *Readings in child development and behavior modification*. Belmont, CA: Brooks/

Cole, 1969; L. A. Penner & M. C. Dertke [Eds.], *Social psychology: The student's reader.* Reading, MA: Addison-Wesley, 1972; G. R. Lefrancois [Ed.], *A survey of child development.* Belmont, CA: Wadsworth, 1974; G. Marin [Ed.], *Lecturas de psicologia social contemporanea.* Mexico: Trillas, 1976.)

With D. Ross & S. A. Ross. A comparative test of the status envy, social power, and secondary reinforcement theories of identificatory learning. *Journal of Abnormal and Social Psychology,* 1963, *67,* 527–534. (Reprinted in, A. W. Staats [Ed.], *Human learning.* New York: Holt, Rinehart & Winston, 1964; P. F. Secord & C. Backman [Eds.], *Problems in social psychology.* New York: McGraw-Hill, 1965; J. F. Rosenblith & W. Allinsmith [Eds.], *The causes of behavior.* II. Boston: Allyn & Bacon, 1966; Y. Brackbill & G. G. Thompson [Eds.], *Behavior in infancy and early childhood.* New York: Free Press, 1967; R. S. Lazarus & E. M. Opton [Eds.], *Readings in personality.* London: Penguin Books, 1967; N. S. Endler, L. R. Boulter, & H. Osser [Eds.], *Contemporary issues in developmental psychology.* New York: Holt, Rinehart & Winston, 1968; R. F. Winch & L. W. Goodman [Eds.], *Selected studies in marriage and the family.* New York: Holt, Rinehart & Winston, 1968; G. G. Thompson [Ed.], *Readings in educational research.* New York: Wiley, 1971; O. M. Ewert [Ed.], *Entwicklungspsychologie:* Band I. Cologne: Kiepenheuer & Witsch Verlag, 1972; R. Ofshe [Ed.], *Interpersonal behavior in small groups.* Englewood Cliffs, NJ: Prentice-Hall, 1973; L. Rosen & R. West [Eds.], *A reader for research methods.* New York: Random House, 1973).

With D. Ross & S. A. Ross. Imitation of film-mediated aggressive models. *Journal of Abnormal and Social Psychology,* 1963, *66,* 3–11. (Reprinted in, D. S. Palermo & L. P. Lipsitt [Eds.], *Research readings in child psychology.* New York: Holt, Rinehart & Winston, 1963; D. Byrne & M. L. Hamilton [Eds.], *Personality research: A book of readings.* Englewood Cliffs, NJ: Prentice-Hall, 1966; W. J. Meyer [Ed.], *Readings in the psychology of childhood and adolescence.* Waltham, MA: Blaisdell, 1967; S. Endelman [Ed.], *Violence in the streets.* Chicago: Quadrangle Books, 1968; R. G. Kuhlen [Ed.], *Studies in educational psychology.* Waltham, MA: Blaisdell, 1968; B. L. Kintz & J. L. Bruning [Eds.], *Research in psychology.* Glenview, IL: Scott, Foresman, 1969; R. K. Parker [Ed.], *Readings in educational psychology.* Boston: Allyn & Bacon,

1969; D. Rogers [Ed.], *Readings in child psychology*. Belmont, CA: Brooks/Cole, 1969; F. Rebelsky & L. Dorman [Eds.], *Child development and behavior*. New York: Knopf, 1970; M. Wertheimer [Ed.], *Psychology and social problems*. Chicago: Scott, Foresman, 1970; R. M. Liebert & R. A. Baron [Eds.], *Human social behavior: A contemporary view*. Homewood, IL: Dorsey Press, 1971; K. D. O'Leary & S. G. O'Leary [Eds.], *Classroom management: The successful use of behavior modification*. Oxford: Pergamon Press, 1972.)

With F. W. McDonald. The influence of social reinforcement and the behavior of models in shaping children's moral judgments. *Journal of Abnormal and Social Psychology*, 1963, *67*, 274–281. (Reprinted in, J. M. Seidman [Ed.], *Readings in educational psychology* [2nd ed.]. Boston: Houghton Mifflin, 1965; H. C. Lindgren [Ed.], *Contemporary research in social psychology*. New York: Wiley, 1968; H. E. Fitzgerald & J. P. McKinney [Eds.], *Developmental psychology*. Homewood, IL: Dorsey Press, 1970; K. J. Gergen & D. Marlowe [Eds.], *Personality and social behavior*. Reading, MA: Addison-Wesley, 1970; H. D. Behrens & G. Maynard [Eds.], *The changing child: Readings in child development*. Glenview, IL: Scott, Foresman, 1972; H. Mischel & W. Mischel [Eds.], *Readings in personality*. New York: Holt, Rinehart & Winston, 1973; M. C. Wittrock [Ed.], *Learning and instruction*. Berkeley, CA: McCutchan, 1977.)

The role of imitation in personality development. *Journal of Nursery Education*, 1963, *18*, 207–215.

Behavior theory and identificatory learning. *American Journal of Orthopsychiatry*. 1963, *33*, 591–601. (Reprinted in, R. J. Corsini [Ed.], *Readings in current personality theories*. Itasca, IL: Peacock, 1978.)

With C. L. Winder, F. Z. Ahmad, & L. C. Rau. Dependency of patients, psychotherapists' responses, and aspects of psychotherapy. *Journal of Consulting Psychology*, 1962, *26*, 129–134.

Punishment revisited. *Journal of Consulting Psychology*, 1962, *26*, 298–301. (Reprinted in, G. Balbadelis & S. Adams [Eds.], *The shaping of personality*. Englewood Cliffs, NJ: Prentice-Hall, 1967).

Comments on Dr. Epstein's paper. In M. R. Jones (Ed.), *Nebraska Symposium on Motivation*. Lincoln: University of Nebraska Press, 1962.

Social learning through imitation. In M. R. Jones (Ed.), *Nebraska Symposium on Motivation*. Lincoln: University of Nebraska Press, 1962. (Reprinted, in E. B. Page [Ed.], *Readings for educational psychology*. New York: Harcourt, Brace & World, 1964.)

With D. Ross & S. A. Ross. Transmission of aggression through imitation of aggressive models. *Journal of Abnormal and Social Psychology*, 1961, *63*, 575–582. (Reprinted in, E. D. Evans [Ed.], *Children: Readings in behavior and development.* New York: Holt, Rinehart & Winston, 1968; J. L. Freedman, J. M. Carlsmith, & D. O. Sears [Eds.], *Readings in social psychology.* Englewood Cliffs, NJ: Prentice-Hall, 1971; H. D. Behrens & G. Maynard [Eds.], *The changing child: Readings in child development.* Glenview, IL: Scott, Foresman, 1972; E. Aronson [Ed.], *Readings about the social animal.* San Francisco: Freeman, 1973; E. F. Zigler & I. L. Child [Eds.], *Socialization and personality development.* Reading, MA: Addison-Wesley, 1973; H. Brown & R. Stevens [Eds.], *Social behaviour and experience: Multiple perspectives.* London: Hodder & Stoughton in association with the Open University Press, 1975; B. R. Bugelski [Ed.], *Empirical studies in the psychology of learning.* Indianapolis, IN: Hackett, 1975; J. Willis & D. Giles [Eds.], *Great experiments in behavior modification.* Indianapolis, IN: Hackett, 1976; W. Schonpflug [Ed.], *System Mensch: Beispiele aus der psychologischen fachliteratur.* Stuttgart: Klett-Cotta, 1977.)

With A. C. Huston. Identification as a process of incidental learning. *Journal of Abnormal and Social Psychology*, 1961, *63*, 311–318. (Reprinted in, P. H. Mussen, J. J. Conger, & J. Kagan [Eds.], *Readings in child development and personality.* New York: Harper & Row, 1965, G. R. Medinnus [Ed.], *Readings in the psychology of parent-child relations.* New York: Wiley, 1967; T. D. Spencer & N. Kass [Eds.], *Perspectives in child development: Research and review.* New York: McGraw-Hill, 1970; H. Munsinger [Ed.], *Readings in fundamentals of child psychology.* New York: Holt, Rinehart, & Winston, 1971.)

Psychotherapy as a learning process. *Psychological bulletin*, 1961, *58*, 143–159. (Reprinted in, A. W. Staats [Ed.], *Human learning.* New York: Holt, Rinehart & Winston, 1964; O. Milton [Ed.], *Behavior disorders: Trends and perspectives.* Philadelphia: Lippincott, 1965, [2nd ed.], 1969; R. A. Savage [Ed.], *Readings in clinical psychology.* London: Pergamon Press, 1966; G. E. Stollak, B. G. Guerney, & M. A. Rothberg [Eds.], *Psychotherapy research: Selected readings.* Chicago: Rand McNally, 1966; B. G. Berenson & R. R. Carkhuff [Eds.], *Sources of gain in counseling and psychotherapy.* New York: Holt, Rinehart & Winston, 1967; J. E. Carr & L. Y. Rabkin [Eds.], *Sourcebook in abnormal psychology.* Boston: Houghton Mifflin, 1967; D. S. Holmes [Ed.], *Reviews of research in behavior pathology*. New York: Wiley, 1968; M. Zax & G. Stricker [Eds.], *The study of abnormal behavior* [rev. ed.]. New York: Macmillan, 1969; G. F. Pardo & L. F. Natalacio [Eds.], *La ciencia de la conducta*. Mexico: Editorial Trillas, 1972; L. Bourne & Ekstrand [Eds.], *Principles and meanings of psychology: Readings*. Hinsdale, IL: Dryden Press, 1973; A. C. Kamil & N. R. Simonson [Eds.], *Patterns of psychology: Issues and prospects*. Boston: Little, Brown, 1973; O. Nudler [Ed.], *Problemas epistemologicos de la psichologia*. Buenos Aires, Argentina: Siglo Veintuno Argentina Editores, 1975; L. R. Allman & D. T. Jaffe [Eds.], *Readings in abnormal psychology: Contemporary perspectives*. New York: Harper & Row, 1976.)

With D. H. Lipsher & P. E. Miller. Psychotherapists' approach-avoidance reactions to patients' expression of hostility. *Journal of Consulting Psychology*, 1960, 24, 1–8. (Reprinted in, A. P. Goldstein & S. J. Dean [Eds.], *The investigation of psychotherapy*. New York: Wiley, 1966.)

With R. H. Walters. *Adolescent aggression*. New York: Ronald Press, 1959. (Polish edition, *Agresja w okresie dorastania*, C. Czapow [Trans.], Warszawa: Panstwowe Wydawnictwo Naukowe, 1968.)

With R. H. Walters. Dependency conflicts in aggressive delinquents. *Journal of Social Issues*, 1958, 14, 52–65.

Child-rearing patterns associated with adolescent aggressive disorders. In *Physical and Behavioral Growth*. Columbus, OH: Ross Laboratories, 1958.

Review of *Case studies in childhood emotional disabilities* (Vol. 2) by G. Gardner. *Contemporary Psychology*, 1957, 2, 14–15.

Psychotherapists' anxiety level, self-insight, and psychotherapeutic competence. *Journal of Abnormal and Social Psychology*, 1956, 52, 333–337.

The Rorschach white space response and "oppositional" behavior. *Journal of Consulting Psychology*, 1954, 48, 17–21.

The Rorschach white space response and perceptual reversal. *Journal of Experimental Psychology*, 1954, 48, 113–117.

With A. L. Benton. "Primary" and "secondary'" suggestibility. *Journal of Abnormal and Social Psychology*, 1953, 43, 336–340.

Index

academic achievement. *See* education
Acquired Immune Deficiency Syndrome (AIDS), 77–80
Ader, R., 72
aggression, 6–8, 19–38, 41–48; American Indians and, 36–37; aspects of theory of, 22; Bobo doll experiment, 21–23; dehumanization and, 46; factors contributing to delinquency in children, 21–22; frustration-aggression theory, 7, 37–38; genetics and, 34–35; media influence on, 23–29; moral disengagement and, 41–46; motivators of, 37–38; neurophysiological mechanisms of, 35–36; rape and, 47–48; social factors and, 35; so-ciobiological perspective of, 33–37; theories of, 6–7
Aggression: A Social Learning
AIDS (Acquired Immune Deficiency Syndrome), 77–80
American Indians, 36–37
Ashton, P. T., 65

Bandura, A.: educational background of, 3; personal background and early contributions, 1–7; reactions to criticism, 81–86. *See also* specific topics of study
Bane, A. L., 62
Barchas, J., 70
behavior modification, 8–11; cognitive behavior therapy, 11; environmental determinism,

behavior modification (*cont.*)
10; social cognitive theory, 10,
41, 65–66
Birner, W., 68
Blanchard, E., 15
Bobo doll experiment, 21–23
Bonnell, G., 68
Brouillard, M. E., 70
Brown, S., 71

children, 58–66; development of
academic self-efficacy in, 58–
61; teachers role in development of self-efficacy, 61–66
Cioffi, D., 70
cognitive behavior therapy, 11
cognitive bypass, 83–84
cognitive development, self-efficacy theories of, 58–63
cognitive imagery, health psychology and, 67–68
Cohen, N., 72
collective efficacy, organizational
behavior and, 65–67
Collins, J., 60
Comer, J., 16

DeBusk, R., 73
dehumanization, 46
Delgado, J. M., 35–36
delinquency studies, 21–23. *See
also* aggression
Dembo, M. H., 64
depression, self-efficacy and, 71–
72
Dill, C. A., 62
Dollard, J., 3–4, 15
Donnerberg, R., 68
The Dubliners (Joyce), 55

education, 58–67; academic
achievement and self-efficacy,
60–66; cognitive development
in children, 58–60; teachers'
role in development of self-efficacy in children, 61–66
empowerment model of treatment, 16
endogenous opioids, 70–71
environmental determinism, 10
euphemisms, psychological uses
of, 43–44
Evans, R. I., 62
externalization, 83
Eysenck, H., 11

familial empowerment, 16
Freud, S., 7, 53
frustration, aggression and, 7,
37–38

Garcia, J., 57
genetics, as a factor in aggression, 34–35
Gibson, S., 64
Glaser, R., 68
guided mastery treatment, 16
Guthrie, T. J., 62

Hansen, W. B., 62
Havis, J., 62
health psychology, 67–80; AIDS
issue, 77–80; cardiac rehabilitation, 73–75; cognitive imagery,
67–68; cognitive stressors and
the endogenous opioid system, 70–71; depression, 71–72;
health promotion, 75–77; immune function and expectancy

learning, 72; phobic stressors, 70–71; social support and, 72–75; stress and the immune system, 68–77
Henderson, A. H., 62
Hill, P. C., 62
Holliday, J. E., 68

immunology. *See* health psychology

Jacobsen, L., 59
Joyce, J., 55

Kiecolt-Glaser, J., 68–69
Koelling, R. A., 57

Landenslager, M. L., 69
Lorenz, K., 7

Maier, S. F., 69
Matthews, O. C., 68
Maxwell, S. E., 62
media, 23–32; approaches to decreasing violence in, 30–32; influence on aggression, 23–29
Messick, G., 68
Milgram, S., 45, 47
Miller, A., 44
Miller, N. E., 3–4, 15
Mittelmark, M. B., 62
modeling, 4–6; functions of, 5
moral development, 39–50; social cognitive theory of, 41
moral disengagement, 41–46; advantageous comparison, 42; dehumanization and, 46; euphemistic language and, 43–

44; moral justification, 42; social level of, 48–50
motivation, self-efficacy and, 54

neurophysiological mechanisms of aggression, 35–36
nuclear deterrents, 49–50

O'Leary, A., 71
organizational behavior, 65–67; social cognitive theory and, 65–66

Parker, L., 65
Patterson, J., 16
phobias, 12–13, 70–71; phobics and self-efficacy, 70–71
Pierce, G. R., 72
plasticity, definition of, 33
Principles of Bahavior Modification (Bandura), 8
"Psychoanalysis Determinable, Indeterminable" (Freud), 53
psychoneuroimmunology, 67–80. *See also* health psychology
"Pygmalion in the Classroom" study, 59–60

Raines, B. E., 62
rape, 47–48
rejection, 55–57
Rejection (White), 55
Ricker, D., 68
Ritter, B., 15
Romisher, S. C., 68
Rosenthal, R., 59
Ross, D., 22
Ross, S., 22
Rozell, R. M., 62

Rubin, D. B., 59
Ryan, S. M., 69

Sarason, B. R., 72
Sarason, I. G., 72
Schunk, D., 59
self-efficacy, 51–80; academic achievement and, 60–66; cognitive development and, 58–63; collective efficacy and organizational functioning, 65–67; depression and, 71–72; development in children, 58–61; effect on motivation, 54; effects on psychological functioning, 54–56; health psychology and, 67–80; phobics and, 70–71; rejection and, 55–57; teachers' perception of, 64–65
self-regulation, capacity for, 34
sexual behavior, AIDS prevention, 77–80
Sheppard, S., 68
Simonton, S., 68
Skinner, B. F., 10
social cognitive theory, 10, 41, 65–66; of moral development, 41; organizational behavior and, 65–66
Social Foundations of Thought and Action (Bandura), 85
Social Learning and Imitation (Miller & Dollard), 3–4, 15

social support and health psychology, 72–75
sociobiological perspective of aggression, 33–37; genetics and, 34–35
Speicher, C. E., 68
Stout, J., 68
Strain, E. C., 68
stress, 68–77. See also health psychology
symbolization, capacities for, 33–34

Tarr, K. L., 68
Taylor, B., 70, 73
teaching, 61–66. See also education
television. See media

vicarious learning, capacities for, 34
violence, 19–38. See also aggression

Walters, R., 21
Watters, J. K., 80
Webb, R. B., 65
White, J., 55
Wiedenfeld, S., 71
Williams, L., 70
Williams, R., 69, 72
Williger, D., 68
Wolberg, L., 11

ABOUT THE AUTHOR

RICHARD I. EVANS is Distinguished Professor of Psychology and Director of the Social Psychology/Behavioral Medicine Research Group at the University of Houston. As a long-time researcher in the social psychology of communications and pioneer in public television, he originated and has since served as director of the Dialogues in Contemporary Psychology Series, originally supported by the National Science Foundation. Beginning with his now classic *Dialogue with C. G. Jung*, he has completed tapes and films and published books based on dialogues with a number of historically significant contributors to psychology, such as B. F. Skinner, Erich Fromm, Carl Rogers, Jean Piaget, Gordon Allport, Erik Erikson, and playwright Arthur Miller.

Dr. Evans's research has led to the origination of the social inoculation model addressed to the prevention of tobacco and other substance abuse among adolescents, which has had substantial impact on research and programs to prevent teenage substance abuse (such as "Just Say No"). Dr. Evans was particularly pleased to complete this volume with Albert Bandura since Bandura's social learning concepts contributed significantly to the development of the social inoculation model.

Dr. Evans has been honored with many significant awards over the years, including the National Phi Kappa Phi Distinguished Scholar Award, various research excellence awards, and a media award from the American Psychological Foundation for a volume in this series.